8/12/21

trout country

trout country
BOB SAILE

REFLECTIONS ON

RIVERS, FLY FISHING &

RELATED ADDICTIONS

PRUETT PUBLISHING COMPANY
BOULDER, COLORADO

Printed in the United States
08 07 06 05 04 03 02 01 00 99   5 4 3 2 1

Library of Congress Cataloging-in-Publication Data

Saile, Bob.
    Trout country : reflections on rivers, fly fishing & related
addictions / Bob Saile.
       p. cm.
    ISBN 0-87108-902-5 (alk. paper)
    1. Trout fishing Anecdotes. 2. Fly fishing Anecdotes. 3. Saile,
Bob. I. Title
SH688.U6S25 1999
799.1'757—dc21   99-36313
                                           CIP

Design by Studio Signorella
Book composition by Lyn Chaffee

To Scott Ratcliff, man of wit and humor,
esteemed friend and perfect streamside companion,
gone from us way too soon.
Scotty, I wish I had known you longer.

"*People often ask me why I enjoy fishing, and I cannot explain it to them because there is no reason in the way they want meanings described. They are asking a man why he enjoys breathing when he really has no choice but to wonder at its truth.*"

—A. J. McClane

"*I am haunted by waters.*"

—Norman Maclean

contents

Preface ix

Acknowledgments. xv

Part One: Roots and Redemption

   1. Chokecherry Heaven 3
   2. Discovery. 11
   3. Home River 21
   4. Hail to the Chief 35

Part Two: Roots and Redemption

   5. Laramie Legacy. 41
   6. San Juan Circus 51
   7. The Born-Again Gunnison 57
   8. The Fork that Roars. 67

Part Three: Roots and Redemption

   9. Mysis Mania 79
   10. The New Ice age. 89
   11. Being There 97

Part Four: Roots and Redemption

   12. Heavy Hitters 107
   13. Counting Coup 115
   14. "My Way or the Highway". 123

Part Five: Roots and Redemption

   15. The Graceful Grayling. 137
   16. Day of the Squawfish 145
   17. Stranger in Steelhead Country. 153
   18. The Great Land 169
   19. High Country. 183

preface

There are 35 million licensed fishermen—anglers, to use a word that suits both sexes and all ages—in this country, and millions more who fish but aren't required to have a license. (To me, there's not necessarily a gender distinction in the word "fisherman," but maybe I'm not as in step with the times as I should be.)

It is interesting to entertain the question of what sets all these people apart in their thinking from the 200 million or more who—by choice and not by limiting circumstance—don't fish.

John Voelker, who wrote under the name Robert Traver, told us in his *Testament of a Fisherman* that it wasn't a case, in his mind, of fishing being so much more important than "the other concerns of men." But if fishing was equally unimportant, he ventured, it was sure as hell a lot more fun. "I fish because I love to," he wrote, "because I love the environs where trout are found, which are invariably beautiful." He went on to list other considerations, including one about bourbon always tasting better out of an old tin cup.

I agree with almost all of what he wrote but have mild reservations about a few parts of his famous testament. One is the supposedly superior quality of bourbon in a tin cup. No reservations about bourbon, mind you, just the tin cup. I'll take my bourbon in a glass, thank you. Also, I don't draw the arbitrary line at trout. I believe that they are the most beautiful and compelling of fish, but game fish are to be respected and sought after whatever the species and wherever they exist, as far as I'm concerned. The bulk of this book is about trout and fly-fishing for trout, but not because I think other species are unworthy of my attention. Moreover, fishing, for any species, is not something I consider unimportant. Anybody who read the late Judge Voelker's considerable contributions to trout-fishing literature knows it was deeply important to him. It was the nucleus of his life. He was pulling our legs a bit with that "unimportant" business.

The quality of fishing that is available to me is a measure of the quality of my life. I have made fishing a more than significant aspect of it, to the point where it has been inseparable from my basic contentment and from my profession as a journalist. I have frequently been asked, "If you had to choose between either fishing or hunting, which one would you choose?" This would be a *Sophie's Choice* sort of recreational dilemma, with an unpalatable option either way. But I would have to take fishing, absolutely. Of course, I would suffer serious hunting withdrawal seizures at specific times of the year, particularly in the spring when the turkeys are gobbling and in the golden days of autumn, when the upland birds beckon. Nevertheless, you can fish all year long in most places, even if you have to do it by drilling your way through a slab of ice.

I fished before I hunted, and I'm sure that I'll fish after I have stopped hunting because of age and infirmity. If what we seek in our outdoor endeavors is connection—connection to the mysteries of the natural world—I cannot imagine better ways to achieve it than in the spontaneity of the strike and the feel of the wildness, strength, and fluidity of a fish transmitted through line and rod. This essential element of fishing does not change from the time we first pick up a pole or a rod to the times we spend pursuing exotic fish in exotic places with the most sophisticated tackle technology can devise. The pleasure, the excitement, and the sense that secrets are being revealed, which I feel on a first-class trout stream, are, at their roots, basically the same as I felt as a kid on a bluegill pond.

The catching of a fish is reassurance to me that I have come to understand how nature works. It is a way of measuring not just my angling skills, but my comprehension of how land and water and the life forces in both are linked in a complicated but beautiful harmony. When I hook a trout or other fish, I have established to my satisfaction that I can comprehend what is happening in a creek, a pond, a river, a lake, a bay, or an ocean. How I react to my challenges, successes, and failures in this endeavor called fishing also tells me a lot about myself. In some way that is not easy to define, some part of me—I suppose it's my soul—is invigorated and restored.

All of which may cause you to say, "Excuse me, but that's a lot of pretentious bullshit." Maybe so. To the extent that the preceding paragraph may be interpreted as some self-indulgent writer claiming there is a higher purpose to fishing than catching fish, it probably should be labeled bullshit. There are other purposes, but if we don't fish for the fun of catching, we have lost sight of the main point.

That still leaves the question of why this sort of fun is more enjoyable and satisfying and meaningful than, say, a day of bird-watching with the local Audubon chapter or going bowling with the boys. Among the reasons, I think, are the physical link with the fish and the conviction that you are one step closer to the answers you seek in nature. This is gauged partly by the relative difficulty of capturing the fish and by the fish's size, strength, beauty, and fighting qualities—and yes, even its culinary qualities if killing and eating the fish are proper and natural in the context of the particular fishing experience and the resource. There is nothing more intimate in nature than the relationship between predator and prey. Fishing, though it has evolved into a necessary catch-and-release ethic for many species, is still a blood sport, because the creatures into which you sink hooks are flesh and blood.

There is a fly-fisherman and flytier of some renown who not so long ago was promoting the use of hooks without points. Not hooks without barbs, mind you—many fishermen have taken to using barbless hooks at least some of the time—but hooks without points, hooks that end in another eye where the point should be.

This gentleman may well have been playing a sly little joke (he is known for an unusual sense of humor), with his tongue comfortably nestled in his cheek, but he was saying that hooks without points constituted the ultimate conservation technique in heavily fished waters, particularly trout waters. The angler could have the satisfaction of seeing or feeling the strike, and maybe of watching the fish bolt or jump, while knowing that he was able to fool it. But he would avoid causing the fish pain or injury or, in some cases, eventual death even if it were released.

Incredulously, I heard a professional wildlife manager in Arizona postulate to me essentially the same approach regarding elk hunting. He proposed issuing permits in high-demand, limited-entry elk-hunting areas that would allow only the use of "paint-ball" guns. The hunter would stalk or bugle in his elk, then fire a projectile that would splash a paint blotch on the animal's body. Tag, you're it—no harm, no foul.

Sorry, guys, but that's not what it's all about—not to me, anyway. There is no hunt without the possibility of a kill. There is no angling without the possibility of a hooked fish. I want to feel the fish for more than a fleeting moment, comprehend physically the vibrancy of it, test it and test my reflexes against its determination to free itself, touch it, admire it. Even if all I do in the end is carefully release it. And most of the time, with many species of fish, that's what I do.

But I don't want to insult the fish—or the elk. I don't want to diminish its dignity anymore than I already have simply by inserting myself into its existence in the first place. Splashing paint all over the side of an elk is a degradation of the animal—graffiti in the great outdoors. If you have no desire to kill this animal, why are you acting out what amounts to a charade? If you have no interest in capturing, even temporarily, this fish that you are interrupting in its daily struggle for survival, why the hell are you bothering it in the first place?

At another extreme is the science-will-render-all-fish-to-possession approach. While an understanding of the fish's world is a satisfying key to success and enjoyment in fishing, fishing cannot and should not be reduced to a scientific blueprint. Sport fishing today, in many instances, has been confused and even perverted by all sorts of technologically based commandments, the gist of which is that if you have the hot new fly or lure, the best rod and reel, the sleekest boat, the most sensitive sonar, the strongest, thinnest monofilament, the precise scientific game plan, and the stylish logo patches all over your jacket, you are bound to be a stud duck among your piscatorial peers. ("Be the first on your block to tear 'em up with an electronic crankbait, Bubba.") In the mumbo jumbo of the prophets of these scientific covenants, all that stands between you and a forty-fish day are your checking-account balance and your inability to boil everything down to a precise formula. In this approach, happiness on the water is as exact as the steps in a chemistry-lab experiment.

That, friends, IS bullshit. The application of technology and science is only a part of it—a fascinating and helpful part if you care to study it, but not the most important part. Because the only person you really need to satisfy, to please, to impress, is yourself. And you can do that in the world of sport fishing—with or without the latest, most expensive gizmos and the by-the-book game plans—by simply following your instincts and your observations, the compulsions that take you on this quest called fishing. And it doesn't require electronic lures, a pH meter, a vocabulary of Latin entomological labels, or a chart of the precise measurements of mayfly body segments (although a basic understanding of insect hatches sure as hell helps in fly-fishing). Nor does it require a forty-fish day, or even a four-fish day. There is some truth in the shop-worn homily that if we always caught fish, fishing would be somewhat dull (although I would certainly like to try it for a few months).

The subjective twisting of sporting ethics and the arbitrary application of personal angling-method preferences also confuse the issue. The man who enjoys catching his fish with a dead-drift nymph doesn't need to be told by the dry-fly purist that he is missing the aesthetic boat. The man who is adept and happy with a spinning rod may be missing out on the joys of fly-fishing, but that doesn't make him a clod or a brute. Within the bounds of regulations and legal tackle, sportsmanship and conservation are in the man, not the method. We are more consequential, more effective, in our bond as anglers than we are as proponents of our subjective differences in approach.

As Roderick Haig-Brown wrote, "The pleasures of angling are many, and they have many sources." Fishing takes you to beauty and involves you with places and people and events that will not only be remembered, but cherished. A life spent fishing is a journey, a search.

All the answers to the question of what sets fishermen apart from those who don't choose to fish are as elusive as an old brown trout inspecting and rejecting the perfect float of your fly, or the last glint of sundown light reflected off the surface of a silken river. Those who have the opportunity to fish, but don't, are content to know the fish are there, whether or not they ever see them, feel them, connect with them, or possess them. Either that, or they don't give a damn whether the fish are there or not.

Fishermen do give a damn and are not content unless they can make the effort at connection. I suggest, as I continue in this quest for fish and describe some of it—the fish, the people, and the places—in this book that the core difference between those who don't fish and those who do is as simple as this: Those who do fish are especially blessed.

Bob Saile
Englewood, Colorado
November 1999

ACKNOWLEDGMENTS

An attempt to acknowledge everybody who helped me with the experiences and learning that formed the background of this book would require a separate chapter. The names of several of these people appear in the book—friends, mentors, and long-time fishing companions. Some aren't named in the book, but they are by no means unappreciated, much less forgotten. To all of them, I extend my profound thanks.

Appreciation also should be expressed to the professional men and women who work in fish-management capacities for state wildlife agencies, persons who generously assisted over the years with the gathering of facts.

Thanks go too, to my daughter Sharla, who gave her time in the computer preparation of the manuscript while patiently accepting my excuses for being a computer klutz. And to Jim Pruett, who had faith in the manuscript. And to the editors of the *Denver Post*, who made it possible over many years for me to sample the great waters of the Rocky Mountain West and other regions.

Finally, there is no way to acknowledge in one sentence or page the wonderful gifts of trout and other game fish and the waters in which they are found. My hope is that this book will convey at least a measure of my deep love and appreciation for these resources.

PART one
ROOTS&
REDEMPTION

CHAPTER 1

CHOKECHerrY Heaven

TAN-COLORED CADDIS FLIES SCATTER LIKE SELF-PROPELLED CON-fetti from the streamside brush as I push through to the green-tea flow of the Eagle River. Mosquitoes whine around my ears, convincing me to stop and extract a spray can of dope from a fly-vest pocket. But I don't mind. Mosquitoes and caddis are the harbingers of early summer on a Colorado trout stream, and the bug life bodes well for an afternoon of fly-fishing.

My fishing partner, a Bureau of Land Management (BLM) field supervisor I met only today, has disappeared upstream. His jeep is parked at a fence gate about one hundred yards back through the sagebrush flat. He just finished guiding me on a tour of the juniper-dotted, aspen-groved ridges high over the river canyon, where he showed me a scattering of hay-bale dams on tributary creeks and draws.

The makeshift straw dams were placed there under super-vision of the BLM, which hopes to stem the tide of erosion on what I consider to be overgrazed slopes—summer range for sheep and cattle. The BLM man went through an earnest spiel about conservative range-rotation practices, but I have my doubts, and I am more interested in the hoped-for secondary blessings of the crude dams—a check on the gushes of mud that cascade down these draws to the river when summer rainstorms hit. The Eagle below any of these chalky spurts turns cocoa colored every time it happens.

The BLM man has taken us to a spot on the river upstream from the worst of the chalky tributaries, which makes me wonder how well the check dams are working. No matter, a bright summer day like this is too promising to waste on range-management debate when a trout stream beckons, and all I want from the remainder of this day is a few feeding fish. The Eagle, just a few highway miles west of the ski-resort sprawl of Vail, is one of those obscure trout rivers that doesn't get talked about much outside the boundaries of Colorado. It flows through a channel of troubles—mining pollution high up in its headwaters; a wall-to-wall spreading of condos, ski areas, golf courses, and assorted rich-folk getaways in the Eagle Valley; the siltation problem on the lower end (which hurts both the anglers and the trout, the latter especially during spawning); and a general dearth of public access on the best stretches. Fly-fishermen occasionally joke about the "golf-ball hatch" on the stream sections just downstream from the playgrounds for the rich and famous. It is not unusual to look down around your wader-clad feet and see a golf ball or two tumbling by in surrealistic suspension just above the bottom rocks.

But we are on private ranch property, and, once away from the parallel highway, the Eagle here looks to be just what I know it can be on a good day—a beautiful, medium-size, primarily pocket-water river with a surprisingly good population of trout (mostly browns but with a decent representation of rainbows).

I swing out around the thickest of the streamside cover, then duck back in toward the water to emerge on a small, gravelly beach just downstream from a bend. At the elbow of the bend on my side of the river, there is a drop-off bottom ledge tight to a bank overhung with a large chokecherry bush. There is a slick below the ledge, and the branches of the bush overhang the right-hand side of the slick.

The reasonably clear water and the presence of the moth-like caddis flies have moved me to choose a dry fly, and I muddle over my possibilities: An Elk Hair Caddis seems the obvious choice, but I may be the only angler in the West who thinks the Elk Hair pattern is overrated. I have always had more success during caddis surface feeding with a small Letort Hopper, which, with its downwing configuration, looks as much like a caddis to me as a grasshopper. But for some reason, I pass on both the Elk Hair and the Hopper and reach for a No. 14 Adams.

The Adams has always been a trustworthy pattern on the Eagle, and it is general enough to pass for a brownish-gray caddis, yet is mayfly-specific enough to look like a Green Drake, which can also be hatching in July. Besides, precisely matching the hatch isn't a priority in my mind on this day. The idea is simply to see a trout or two rise to a floating fly after months of winter and spring nymphing in cold or murky currents. The long spring runoff has surrendered its seasonal grip reluctantly.

Even before I can get the Adams tied to my 5X tippet, I catch a glimpse from the periphery of my vision—a flashy splash almost underneath the chokecherry branches. A brown has snatched something off the surface. The "brush hatch" of caddis is sending the egg-laying insects out over the surface, dipping and then lifting off again quickly, as if the water is hot to their touch. My fingers begin to quiver, and it takes longer than it should to tie the clinch knot.

Another quick splash out from the branches, and a fluttering caddis is no longer there. I wade out into ankle-deep water downstream from the rises, strip out the No. 5 floating line, letting a few coils of it drop around my legs, then stare hard at the slick along the bushy overhang. The water can be no more than two feet deep there, but the shadows of the brush and the slight turbidity of the water make it impossible to tell how many trout might be there or how big they might be. The spot looks too small for a concentration of fish, and I begin to wonder if I might be dealing with a lone brown that has made the slack water below the ledge his personal hidey-hole.

The back cast is tricky because there is a dead juniper snag over my right shoulder, and it will require a fair imitation of a Lefty Kreh–type maneuver to cast from the edge of the sandy beach. I bear scant resemblance to Lefty Kreh, with or without a rod in my hands, so I slosh carefully out into deeper water to give myself some back-cast room. The bottom is bowling balls coated with crude oil, or so it always seems on the Eagle.

Depth perception and distance gauging never have been my strong suits, and with my first upstream cast, I hang the Adams in the tip of a branch. Luckily, it pulls loose easily and skitters across the slack water as I pull it back for another cast. I think I see a flash of yellow color beneath the fly as it passes out from the branch, but I'm not sure.

The fourth cast finally lands the still-fluffy Adams at the lip of the ledge. There is plenty of slack in the leader and in the twenty feet of fly line that is on the water, and as I crouch, stooped over like a heron to keep my silhouette low, the fly floats two feet downstream and disappears in a swirl.

When I come up on the rod, the brown tries to bolt under the overhanging branches, but I put enough pressure on it to discourage that ploy. I don't much care if I lose this fish—the important thing is the first dry-fly take of the season—but I don't necessarily want to have it wrap me up in sticks or roots.

The fight carries out into the main current and the brown jumps in that wild, absolutely reckless way that browns have early in the fight. I see it is a rather modest-size fish—maybe thirteen inches. It looks good, though—really good.

Moments later, I have its black-and-red-spotted side flashing back at me in the glint of water-reflected sunlight. I extract the fly from the top jaw and slide the fish out of my hand into the flow. The first surface-take trout of the summer is in the books, and this pleases me. The rest will be in the gravy category now. And I know there is more to come, because the river and the day have that look, that feel.

I squeeze out a dab of dry-fly powder from a plastic bottle and dip the sodden Adams into it a few times. The granular chemical does its job, and I am ready for another cast.

I haven't noticed another rise in the spot where I hooked the brown, but I have the sense that another trout is holding there. It's just too promising an ambush point for the fish—proximity to the caddis-bearing bushes and an interception position for the current-carried food items that may tumble over the bottom ledge.

The slashing rise that comes on the very next cast and drift is not expected, however, and I almost miss the fish. I haven't even visually picked up the position of the floating Adams when I see the splash. But I set the hook, and the trout is there, and it's bigger than the other one. The fight is stronger and longer, but the result is the same. The trout is, in fact, a sixteen-inch brown, measured quickly against the butt end of my eight-and-a-half-foot graphite rod, then released.

Two trout on successive casts—not too shabby for starters, I exult, shifting my wading shoes on the slickness of the silt-covered rocks and almost sliding off balance. I recover and reach for more dry-fly powder, and out of the corner of my eye I see another swirl almost under the chokecherry bush.

The wind has begun to gust, and my first efforts at placing the Adams tight to the almost surface-dragging branches go far astray. Finally, a cast lands almost where I want it to, but it sails too far on the extension of a tight line loop and snags in the tip of an overhanging branch. This time, I manage to pop it gently free from the single leaf in which it has lodged, and the Adams plops straight down into the water as if it were a caddis jumping from bush to destiny. Immediately, it is engulfed. This is a better fish yet, and I almost don't lever it out from under the bush before it is hopelessly tangled in the shrubbery. But I do, and I flounder out closer to midstream to get a better angle on the fish after it leaps once, perilously close to the streamside growth. It looks much bigger than it is, as they always do when they jump, but it is plenty big enough.

This brown does a pretty fair imitation of a rainbow, leaping again when it dashes into the midriver current, and for awhile it is close to taking me into the backing. My rod wrist is actually starting to ache a bit when I back up carefully and slide it onto the gravelly beach. It is every bit of seventeen inches.

As I release the trout, it occurs to me that I have had entire afternoons on the Eagle with less excitement than I have just enjoyed in barely more than fifteen minutes. I am on a roll, the river is on a roll, the angling gods are in their piscatorial palace and smiling benevolently down on me.

Beginning to feel like a Vegas casino crapshooter who is tossing nothing but naturals, ready and willing to push his luck, I decide I may as well make a few more casts to this incredible spot. I see no more rises, but there is still one potential holding lie that I haven't covered with my casts, and it's the seam farther out from the bush between the primary current and the protected slick. I don't really believe that there's another trout in this little area, much less one that conforms to the size-progression escalation that seems to be the order of the day, but I'm about ready to believe anything.

The wind is beginning to pick up, and it takes me several casts to place the Adams precisely on a drift course down the current seam. It bobs along for a bit, when suddenly I realize that I can no longer see it. Just for insurance, I lift the rod and—wonder of wonders—there is life. Life, indeed: This brown looks huge as it launches itself stiff-sided out of the water. It crashes back and runs for the bushes. At the same instant that I figure this fantasy will end with the pop of the leader tippet, the fish suddenly decides that its salvation lies out in the main river, in the swiftest flow. When it gets there, I almost conclude that the fish's instinct was correct. Another jump and a downstream run with full support of the current, and I am looking at the beginning of the fly-line backing. But there is nothing out there but water, deep water. No snags, no bushes, just the feel of the current and the panicked fish. There are several moments when the party seems over, but I gradually gain back half the line, wrist definitely aching now. The rest is fairly cut-and-dried.

I slide twenty inches of male brown into the inch-deep water along the little beach. It is a survivor of years of semipolluted water, of the stress of development and the pressure of fishing, and of the silt that tries to choke it to death. I extract the fly, place the rod on the gravel parallel to the edge of the water, and put the trout on its side next to the rod, with the trout still lying in the water that is too shallow to cover it. I want a photo of this fish before I release it—something besides my memory to reassure me years later that any of this ever happened. But just as I reach for the camera around my neck, the brown does the automatic, convulsive flop that always ensues at such moments. I've pushed my luck, and I know it. The trout belly-snakes quickly into water deep enough to give it purchase, and I watch it dart away toward the center of the river.

I pick up the rod and stagger happily over to the grassy bank, where I sit down and light a cigar. It is still hard to believe this little series of unlikely events—four brown trout thirteen to twenty inches taken from one small place consecutively on the same dry fly on a stream where a fifteen-incher is a big fish.

If I don't fish anymore at all today, it won't matter much. But as I look out over the width of the river, out into the mid-channel currents, it dawns on me that the water is now pocked with rises. There are none by the chokecherry bush, but something has moved a lot of trout—a dozen or more—to take up feeding stations across the main flow. Grinning, I powder-dry the Adams and prepare for more of this unexpected bonanza.

Twenty minutes later, I have one eight-inch rainbow to add to my resume. Swallows are crisscrossing the river, darting after whatever is exciting the trout. The trout are still rising, and everybody seems to be making connections except me. Finally, the edges of frustration setting in, I stop casting to try to figure out what the hell is going on. And it's not caddis. The ever-increasing vortexes of the rise-forms are not the slashing takes of trout trying to nab nervous caddis, but the deliberate porpoising movements of mayfly-dun feeding. Now that my eyes are really looking, I see what appears to be a Pale Morning Dun (PMD) hatch—bugs about size 16. I tie on a corresponding pattern and get three straight false rises. Finally, I manage to calm myself long enough to capture one of the natty little insects riding the surface film near the bank, and it is not a PMD. It is a pinkish-brown mayfly, and I realize that I am staring at a Western Red Quill.

This is great. I've figured out the entomological imperative, except for one small matter—I don't have a single Red Quill in my fly boxes. Either I've run out of the pattern or somehow have misplaced my supply. It is not a hatch I see on my home water, the South Platte, and I use it only intermittently on the other streams I fish regularly. I have a vague recollection that Red Quills can be an important hatch on the Eagle in July, but I've failed to plan this time for the contingency. Now I'm about to pay the tab. I have met the enemy, and I am it.

For another hour, I run through a succession of patterns hoping to make do, but I don't, with the exception of one more gullible, ten-inch rainbow. The old standby Adams, even in size 16, is useless. And I'm back down to earth, feet planted solidly in the sands of humility.

There is a theory that presentation, if it is perfect, outshines pattern every time. I sit there, stoking up another cigar, and think: It's a nice theory, but you could have fooled me. I have long since divested myself of the notion that anything I do is perfect, for one thing. And I sure as hell am not fooling these trout, my glorious interlude with the Adams and the spot under the chokecherry bush notwithstanding. And that, I finally decide, is what this fishing fixation is about, this search for personal satisfaction on the waters of the world. In a sense, the river and the trout have redeemed themselves, because very little in fishing is automatic, and it is definitely not always easy. Sometimes it's as difficult as making a box of Red Quills magically appear in a fly vest that doesn't hold any.

Success and failure. Chokecherry Heaven and back down to Mother Earth. The fun of trying. The unpredictability of it. You just never know. But you have been happily trying to find out ever since your angling roots.

CHAPTER 2

Discovery

AS FAR BACK AS I CAN REMEMBER, I'VE BEEN MESMERIZED BY water, preferably moving water but always water that holds fish—especially trout. But not necessarily trout; all game fish are worthy.

It seems to me there are two kinds of fishermen—those who construct their lives, in some significant measure, around the quest for fish, and those who fish only when they can't think of something else to do and their lives are not the least complicated by going fishing. I have always counted myself in the first category, whether being in it was complicated or not.

Fishermen who say they fish not for the fish, but just to "be on the water" or "just because I love to get out" are being somewhat dishonest, I think—or at least self-deceptive and misleading. Or they are not truly fishermen. I cannot envision the purveyors of these just-glad-to-get-out platitudes standing in a sterile, fishless stream or lake and waving a rod all day.

I'd probably spend some time around the water if no fish were in it, but certainly not hours or days at a time. If fish were somehow gone from the water, one of water's more compelling mysteries would be absent, too. There would be much less to contemplate and, to me, little foundation for establishing intimacies with a river or other body of water.

In recent years—they are usually soothingly labeled the "silver years"—I've found that I don't get quite as disappointed with not catching fish as I used to. I know that my angling days are numbered. Everybody's are, but my number is getting smaller than a lot of others. So the act of fishing is a reward in itself. In that sense, I'm just glad to get out, too. Nevertheless, the fire still burns, I still want to catch fish, and I still have trouble not fishing when I'm around the places that hold fish.

My wife says she sometimes wonders why I haven't been killed in a car wreck. Whenever she has been with me as I drive along a stream or by the shores of a lake, her repetitive plea to me, uttered at least once every couple of miles like a prayer, is, "Watch the road, not the water." Or, "You look at the highway, I'll look for rising fish."

The enigmas of water that hold fish have taken me to far-flung places. But the obsession, if that's what it is, began at home in a tiny and unlikely milieu.

I was a grade-school youngster in a neighborhood on the northwest outskirts of Houston, where postwar frame houses had just been built in a pine and oak forest cut by a bayou and its tributaries. In those days, if you lived on the edge of town, you lived on the "outskirts." Today, you live in the "suburbs," but when my family moved in, that word was not yet in the common lexicon.

The first body of moving water I ever fell in love with was a ditch. Actually, the ditch was a small, partly channelized tributary creek of White Oak Bayou. The developers of our subdivision, called Garden Oaks, had left it pretty much in its natural state in some places. Years later, the requisites of progress would force the complete filling in of the creek along its entire length, but in my first few years in our new home, the creek (ditch) was inhabited by fair numbers of sunfish and bullhead catfish. The first fish I ever caught was one or the other, but I don't remember which. Alas, I'm not one of those who can tell you the exact species, length, and girth of my first fish. I do remember, quite clearly, the setting.

There was a timbered bridge over a gravel road that ran past the small corner grocery store. The creek slowed and meandered under the bridge and curved around to pass behind the grocery store, and the deepest water in the creek was on either side of and under the bridge. Looking down into that shadowy place under the bridge, I knew without a doubt that there were revelations that could be conveyed to me only by what lived beneath the surface. And the finest of the things that lived there—the most beautiful— were the fish.

We neighborhood Huck Finns used to perch on the edge of the bridge planking with our legs dangling over the side. Our braided-string fishing lines, tied to cane or willow poles, dangled into the water. The rest of the tackle consisted of a cork sliced with a notch, to be slipped onto the line, and below that, a small bait hook dressed with a grasshopper or a garden worm.

I can still see the pale cork dancing a convulsive jig at the first tentative touches of a pumpkinseed or a bluegill, then diving downward into the greenish-brown murkiness of the water. This dance was an affirmation that the answers about the relationships and responses of living things were there, under the surface, if you asked the right questions. Of course, I didn't frame it in those terms then; I just wanted to reduce something with fins to possession. It took me some time to summon the sense and the patience to wait until I couldn't see the cork anymore before setting the hook.

That was my first lesson in timing the strike.

There was a kid named W. L.—in Texas, it was and still is fairly common for kids to be called by their initials—who never used a cork bobber. He just made it his business to get to the bridge first in the morning so he could position himself over the deepest water, which was directly under the edge of the bridge. He'd then drop his bait straight down, much as an angler would do today if he were vertically jigging. W. L. knew he had a fish when he saw his line twitch or when he felt the tug of the striking fish.

"How in the heck can he catch all those fish without a cork?" was a frequent, puzzled comment from those who observed W. L. in action for the first time.

That was my first lesson in strike detection without the use of a strike indicator.

For two or three years, we fished for the fish, and sometimes, using bacon on a string, for the crayfish of the creek.

But then came a drought, a rare event in the semitropical environs of Southeast Texas, and the ditch temporarily dried up. We went down with our pails and coffee cans and rescued as many sunfish and bullheads from the remaining puddles as we could, then dumped them into a small fish pond that one of the neighbor kids had in his backyard. We were going to take them back and put them in the ditch when the rains came again, but the fish died in the pond because the water lacked the biological necessities that they had in their ditch.

That was my first lesson in failed fish management.

Finally, as the neighborhood grew, Garden Oaks was no longer the last subdivision before you got into the mostly undeveloped woods. All the streets that consisted initially of gravel or oyster shell were paved, and the creek was totally filled in, thus eliminating the need for the bridge—which was removed.

And that was my first lesson in habitat destruction.

The homily is that those who don't learn from history are doomed to relive it. In a sense, though, many of us go through life trying to relive the best parts of our history. We are lucky if we bring it off. I learned some wonderful things from those early days and was later blessed with being able to repeat them on a larger scale—an enduring love for fish and the waters they inhabit, a modest (and on rare days, insightful) ability to catch them, and, most of all, a deep appreciation for the resource and the opportunity.

I was destined, too, to revisit the sadness I had felt at the loss of our neighborhood fishery. There would be times, in years to come, when I would see fish management fail and times when I would see the degradation or destruction of fish habitat. I would also see men triumph in some instances over the insidious threat of those things as we began to truly give a damn about the resources, and as conservation efforts became mobilized and more effective in the form of countless individuals and organizations who cared enough to do something.

I fished a variety of places in ensuing childhood and teenage years, wherever and whenever my father or my friends' fathers or later, teenage friends who had access to cars, could or would take me. But it was not until I set eyes upon a spring-fed creek in the pine and oak forest northeast of Houston that I really became fascinated once again with a particular body of moving water.

Its name was Caney Creek. Actually, there were two creeks—Peach and Caney. Peach was the smaller of the two. They came together about a mile down a two-track rut road from a gate and fence that enclosed a tract of private land between the fence and the forks. An old man who was a patriarch of the family who owned the land used to sit in a little shed just behind the gate, where a misspelled sign proclaimed, "PRAVITE PROP.—FISHING, $1."

I first heard of this mystical place when a fish-crazy teenage friend of mine named Bill sidled up to me one day at high school and, in his most seductive, secretive whisper, conveyed two words: "Peach Creek." (He might have been the guy whispering "plastics" to Dustin Hoffman in *The Graduate*.)

"Huh?"

"Peach Creek," Bill hissed. Bill was a steadfast believer in the proposition that everybody was out to steal everybody else's fishing hole and that the one sure guarantee of not catching fish was to tell somebody else where they could be caught. I was one of the few close buddies for whom he was willing to make an exception.

"My dad has been catching bass at Peach Creek," he said with reverential emphasis on the word "bass." In fact, he said, his dad was catching lots of them in Peach Creek at and near the forks, and in Caney Creek farther downstream.

"What on?" I asked, thinking live minnows, probably.

Bill squinted and looked around shiftily. Nobody was nearby, but he kept whispering anyway. "Hot Rods," he confided.

"Huh?"

"Hot Rod spoons, man. Haven't you heard of 'em?"

"Oh," I said, "sure." Actually, I hadn't heard of them. In fact, I had seldom caught fish on an artificial lure. At that stage of my fishing life, bait was the only sure way to catch any fish, and lures were in a mysterious world that I hadn't entered confidently— at least not yet.

All through boyhood, I had been torn between a feeling of awe when I saw one of my elders casting lures with a bait-casting rod or flies with a fly rod, and a sneaking suspicion that they were just indulging a mostly unproductive affectation. Still, I recently had acquired a functional bait-casting outfit, and it was perfectly capable of casting lures as small as a quarter ounce.

A few days later, Bill showed me a Hot Rod spoon. It was a silver-finish, teardrop-shaped spoon with a single red eye at the head end. As I learned later, it was made by the Les Davis Company and was fairly popular in the northwestern United States as a steelhead lure.

After much planning, plotting, and hoarding of dimes and quarters to purchase a few more Hot Rods, we buttonholed a high-school buddy who had a driver's license and even a car and talked him into a predawn drive to the wilds of Peach and Caney creeks—about forty-five miles northeast of town. Houston in those days was indeed a town (as opposed to a big city) of a few hundred thousand folks; today there are several million people, and if you drive forty-five miles northeast of the center of Houston, you are still in the suburbs. The "outskirts" are no longer clear enough to define.

We were not all that certain, as it turned out, how to get to the hotspot. In the predawn darkness, we ended up on a dirt road through the pines. It was lined by a few small frame "shotgun" houses—I have no idea how that term came into use—occupied by black farm and lumber-mill workers and their families. This was true poverty, and in those days, there were no food stamps.

Lawrence, the other kid—we were all fifteen to sixteen years of age—drove us up to one of the shotgun houses. We walked with concocted bravado up onto the small porch and knocked on the door to ask for directions. The eastern sky was barely turning silver, and there were no lights on in the house.

I held my breath, half expecting to hear a loud boom that would be literally connected with a "shotgun" house. But the man who came to the door was unarmed and looked more scared than we were; he was not used to white folks rousting him out at 5 A.M., and if it had ever happened before, it probably wasn't for something as innocuous as directions to a fishing hole. The middle-aged man graciously gave us our bearings, pointing farther down the road in the direction of the creeks. He even grinned when he saw that we were just kids. The old man who collected the one-dollar fishing toll at the fence gate wasn't on duty yet. We parked the car outside the fence—the gate was locked—and put a note under the windshield wiper saying we would pay on the way out. As we were later to rudely discover, the one dollar charge applied to each person, not to each car, and the three-dollar total charge came within $1.50 of breaking us.

That was my first lesson in fee fishing.

We walked the mile down to the forks, carrying our new-fangled glass bait-casting rods (the era of fiberglass had started only about a decade earlier) with their fancy level-wind reels and dacron line. It was full daylight by the time we made our first casts into Peach Creek just above the forks. The creek flowed clear through a backdrop of long-leaf pine and Spanish moss–draped oaks. A light, early-morning fog hung in the low places.

With breathless expectation, I blew the first two attempts at casting toward the shadowy depths of the far bank, having to pluck out backlashes both times. When I finally got the lure out and across and cranked it back, I was amazed to see a bass following it like a miniature shark closing in on its prey. To this day, I can clearly envision the fish speeding up with fluid quickness and engulfing the lure, turning away with it so aggressively that even my belated raising of the rod tip was enough to set the hook. The strike was mercurial, spontaneous magic, and it seemed to me that the tea-colored flow of the river represented another world, a separate dimension from which the bass had reached out and made a connection. The whole sequence had the feel of prophesy and enchantment.

Later, I would tell of the epic battle of this fourteen-inch beauty with the jagged, splotchy stripes down its sides and the single dark spot at the base of its tail. In reality, I probably just cranked as hard as I could and jerked the fish up on the sandy bank. There are no epic battles with fifteen-pound-test line and fourteen-inch fish.

The little silver spoon with its red eye was hooked solidly into the corner of the jaw of the bass. I was hooked forever, too, on artificial lures—and bass. Later, it would primarily be flies and trout, but in East Texas, bass were often called "green trout" because they were the closest thing we had to trout.

I promptly grabbed the bass, removed the lure, and strung the fish, still flopping, on my cord stringer. None of us had any concept of releasing fish for any reason unless the fish was so small it would be too much bother to clean it and eat it.

That day, we strung up more than a dozen bass before we almost ran out of lures that were lost in water too deep to re-trieve them after they hung up on bottom debris. These beau-tiful bass darted out of the shadowy depths near half-sunken, blow-down logs, or from the recesses of undercut banks or the drop-off edges leading into deeper water. The only places the water was very deep were in scoured-out holes left by the shoveling and digging of a gravel company that had a lease on the creeks. I suppose you could say that was my first lesson in stream improvement.

The creeks were surprisingly clean. They ran with amber clarity over a bed of fine sand, fed by the springs farther up in their forested beginnings. Peach and Caney creeks would be the closest things to a trout stream I would see for another three years.

I didn't think of it that way then, but Caney Creek was my first "home river." It's hard to call a stream a "home river" if you do not have the wherewithal to fish any other rivers of consequence. We went back many times to Caney Creek in the next few years (we eventually found that Peach was too small to be consistently productive), even after the water au-thorities built Lake Houston Dam on the main river farther downstream and Caney Creek began to back up and be-come silty.

We always caught bass, sometimes on spoons and sometimes on lures such as the River Runt, the Bomber, or the Pico Perch, and we always assumed that the fish were largemouth bass. It was not until many years later, when, looking over a bunch of black-and-white snapshots taken on one of our trips, I studied a close-up of a stringer of these small bass (a two-and-a-half-pounder was a lunker) and it dawned on me that they were spotted bass, not largemouths.

Often called Kentucky spotted bass, this particular species of bass has, or at least had, a surprisingly extensive native range in the southern states, stretching all the way from Ohio and Tennessee and Kentucky down into the pine forests of East Texas and over to western Florida. They were stream dwellers initially but spread naturally or by stocking to reservoirs as well. After some research, there was no doubt in my mind that Caney and Peach creeks were part of that native range.

But I was to get my second major shock about what man's "progress" can do to fish habitat. Gradually, the effect of the reservoir downstream, especially when it filled and flooded surrounding timber, was to flood or slow down the creeks and change their water quality. Even in college-age years, we kept fishing Caney Creek occasionally, but eventually, the spotted bass were no longer part of the ecological picture and we had to settle for catfish or crappies or the white bass that ran up out of the lake on their spawning runs in February and March. Finally, when Lake Houston itself declined as a fishery, there was no longer any reason to fish Caney and Peach creeks, and by then the new owners of the land around it didn't allow access, with a fee or otherwise, anyway.

The first trout stream on whose banks I remember standing—up close enough to study it, to feel it, to hear it—was the Firehole River in Yellowstone National Park. This opportunity came on a highway journey from Texas to the white-pine forests of northern Idaho, where I would toil as a blister-rust control "brush ape" for Uncle Sam's Forest Service. It was a job I took during summer break from college. We stopped in the park and stood in a pullout parking spot to gawk at the river. We had no time to fish.

The Firehole was surreal to me, and not just because of the vaporous geysers and hot, sulphurous flows that trickled into its blue currents. That anything this beautiful could actually contain fish, not to mention the mysteriously exquisite trout, seemed fantastic, and I swore that one day I would fish it. One day, I did, but it would be several years later.

That summer, the first trout stream—if you could call it that—I ever fished was a small creek in the timbered ridges near the little lumber town of Elk River, in northern Idaho. The first trout I ever caught was one of the creek's brook trout, an eight-incher that succumbed to a gaudy Parmachene Belle wet fly. I remember placing the little brookie in the streamside grass and staring at it, ogling it, and thinking that there was something ethereal about trout—a conviction that had first come to me after I started poring over trout-fishing stories and photos in the major outdoor magazines. Studying that brook trout, I had a premonition that somehow trout would play a large role in shaping the rest of my life.

More than that, fly-fishing had cast a spell over me. I was certain that taking trout, or any other fish, with a fly rod was the pinnacle of angling. There was artistry and grace in the act of fly-fishing, some mystical melding of the soul of the angler and the method of his madness. That same summer, I would be introduced to the wonders of dry-fly fishing for cutthroats in Marble Creek on Idaho's St. Joe River drainage, although I was severely handicapped by my bulky, bass-weight glass fly rod and the primitive fly line with which I had equipped it.

But I discovered more than trout that summer. I discovered that some day, I had to live in the wonderful country in which they were found. I would need to move West. And eventually, I did.

CHAPTER 3

Home River

SOON AFTER I MOVED TO DENVER IN 1967, IT BECAME CLEAR TO me that trout fishermen along Colorado's Front Range were blessed with perhaps the most productive trout stream in America that was within fifty miles of a major city (not counting steelhead and salmon rivers as "trout streams"). But for roughly three years, my efforts to fish the South Platte River with any degree of success resembled the joustings of a quixotic adventurer lunging at piscatorial windmills.

I remember quite clearly the first day I saw a major hatch of mayflies near the crossroads hamlet of Deckers, about five miles downstream from Cheesman Dam. Trout were breaking the surface all around me in an evenly spaced orgy of feeding. It was impossible to make a cast in any direction without placing a fly over or near a trout.

My No. 14 Ginger Quills and Royal Coachmans and White Millers may as well have been bass plugs for all the good they were doing me. These flies had been purchased at a sporting-goods store with no more clue as to their usefulness than if I had been buying parts for a space rocket. There were innumerable streams and ponds and other waters in Colorado where these patterns would have been adequate to fool a few gullible trout, but the South Platte, as I was learning, was not one of them.

Then somebody said the magic words: "Blue Quill" and "Jim Poor."

I had told my tale of woe to one of the editors at the *Denver Post*, where I was then a city desk reporter, and he happened to be a fly-fisherman. He informed me, after chuckling over my description of my tackle and fly patterns, that I would have to "match the hatch." I comprehended, in general terms, what this phrase meant. But I had no idea what the hatches were on the South Platte, although obviously the bugs were small.

What was hatching during this period in July, although it would be a few years before I could define it in entomological terms, were *Baetis* mayflies, or Blue-Winged Olives. My benefactor at the paper suggested looking up Jim Poor, who owned a small fly shop in an old motel building on South Santa Fe. Poor, he said, was the only guy in town tying and selling flies small enough to match the South Platte hatches, and what I obviously needed for dry-fly fishing were some No. 20 or 22 Blue Quills.

I stood there with my jaw drooping, peering down at what, lying in the palm of my hand, looked like a cluster of tiny, dead, grayish gnats. Jim Poor grinned and said that would be six dollars, please. Never had I seen flies or hooks that small. But I made the purchase, along with a couple of leaders tapered down to 6X. In those days, 6X was about as small, in practical terms, as leader tippets could be, and the state of the art of synthetics was such that 6X was no stronger than today's 7X.

I nail knotted one of these leaders to my bulky, weight-forward floating fly line, coiled up on a Pflueger Medalist single-action reel, which in turn was clamped onto a rod that by today's standards would look like something you would use to beat the dust out of a rug. It was a Heddon glass fly rod built for bass or bluegill fishing, a pole that I had brought up from Texas with me.

Tiny insects were riding the slick surface of the small but deep pool like a regatta of blue-gray sailboats. I had been standing at the edge of the water for several moments, staring down at the sight of brown trout torpedoing the little mayfly boats with relentless efficiency. They did it with the grace of aquatic ballet artists. They were not the least hurried in their purpose. This was happening in a stretch of canyon-enclosed pocket water about a half mile above Lone Rock Campground. A nose, a head, and a dorsal fin would roll with graceful languor up through the surface film, and one of the *Baetis* duns would disappear.

Full of trust in my new supply of Blue Quills, I don't know how many sloppy casts I made before I hooked one of those brown trout. A thirteen-incher happened to be rising in a spot where the little Blue Quill floated for perhaps three seconds before the inevitable drag action would ensue (I knew nothing about the arcane tactics of mending line or other means of extending a drag-free float). It took me a second to realize that the fish had actually eaten *my* fly. This delay probably helped in the hook setting. I would eventually learn that in dry-fly fishing, it sometimes pays to pause a second to give the trout a chance to turn down and away with the fly.

I played that trout about three times as long as was necessary, but as far as I was concerned, I was fishing with a cobweb for terminal tackle. When the trout was in hand, I cracked it over the head with my pocket knife and laid it out on a rock to stare at it. Its golden-yellow hues, splashed with black and red spots, made this fish the most beautiful thing with fins I had ever seen. I wanted to yell in heady triumph, or at least turn around and share this defining moment with someone, anyone. Nobody else was there.

Before the hatch ended, I would put four more brown trout on the rock and then into my creel—in those days, an eight-trout limit was in place on the Deckers water. Today, it is two fish, sixteen inches or better, and catch-and-release in Cheesman Canyon itself, and it has been at least fifteen years since I have killed a trout anywhere near Deckers, whether it was legal or not.

An angler's relationship to his home river (or any river he knows really well) can be likened to the progression of an early-stage love interest into the permanence of marriage or, as we say today, an ongoing "relationship." In angling terms, the river becomes his "significant other." It begins with visual attraction, a longing, a kind of passionate envisionment of intimacy that is signified by tentative, hold-your-breath advances. It is understood, if you comprehend your own limitations, that this initial engagement may not lead to anything immediately. But you definitely want it to. So you keep trying, and maybe you even seek advice about how to proceed. As you get more comfortable with the river and its fish, and it begins to respond (like a woman who at least appreciates the fact that you are interested), you establish the beginnings of rapport. This leads to breaking down the barriers—the restraints that hold back familiarity and consummation. And finally, you are committed to the river and it has surrendered something to you that will always be there for you. Then you begin to learn things about the river and about yourself that can come only with time and faithfulness. You now can claim it as your own. And it can claim you. Thus it was with me and the South Platte.

Within the next few years after my inaugural triumph over the South Platte mystery, I acquired a seven-and-a-half-foot Phillipson bamboo fly rod, among others, and bought a double-taper line and dozens more tiny dry flies from Jim Poor. Sometimes, I would paw through my vest the evening before a planned visit to the river, only to find that my supply of Blue Quills or tiny Poor Witch patterns (similar to a spent-wing Adams and used to match the Trico hatch) was low. I'd telephone Poor to ask if he had some on hand. "I'll tie 'em up and leave 'em in the mailbox for you to pick up," he'd say, knowing that I would be passing the shop too early for him to be open. I usually paid him on the way home.

Jim Poor retired some years later, selling the business, and his little shop was the genesis of Anglers All, just down the road from the now-nonexistent motel.

The South Platte River is born in obscure rivulets high in the rarefied air of the Mosquito Range on the western rim of the vast, lonely, and often windswept South Park Basin. It tumbles down the Middle and South forks, with the upper

Middle Fork coursing past piles of dredged-up rock—the legacy of generations of gold seekers. Today, the pilgrimages to South Park streams are made by fortune seekers dressed in neoprenes and wielding fly rods instead of picks and shovels. The gold they seek is on the sides of brown trout, although there are also big rainbows and Snake River–strain cutthroats to be caught during spring spawning runs out of Antero, Spinney Mountain, and Elevenmile reservoirs.

The river becomes a switchback maze of serpentine bends on the flat, grassy ranchland meadows at Hartsel and below, until it passes through Spinney Dam then plunges out of Elevenmile Dam and enters Elevenmile Canyon itself. From there, the river carves its way through pine-covered ridges and granite outcrops to dump into Cheesman Reservoir, then out again into Cheesman Canyon and down past Deckers and Trumbull.

The hairpin curves in the South Park meadow sections hold mostly modest-sized trout except during spawning periods, when the character of the fishing changes dramatically. Trout weighing up to ten pounds can be hooked by those who know their spawning timetables and the techniques, which usually involve nymph fishing.

Today, there are some thirty miles of South Park streams on both forks and the main stem open to public fishing, largely as a result of an ambitious and expensive acquisition and leasing program by the Colorado Division of Wildlife. Up through the early 1980s, the spawn-run riches were mostly the province of private lease holders or fishing clubs. The late Richard O'Connor of Denver made his reputation as a catcher of trophy trout on his own nine-mile-long lease on the Middle Fork. He plucked these plums from the riffles and undercut runs with a bamboo rod and just a single pattern—a No. 10 Hairwing Rio Grande King wet fly. In these days of heavy public fishing pressure, that pattern on most days would be rudely ignored by all but the smaller, less wary trout. Egg-fly patterns sometimes work during spawning runs, or San Juan Worms and Woolly Buggers, but on a month-in, month-out basis, tiny midge-type nymphs and dry flies will produce more consistently.

The best South Park fishing is found on the three-mile Spinney Ranch section between Spinney Dam and the inlet of Elevenmile Reservoir. Resident trout averaging twelve to eighteen inches are numerous, their presence enhanced and bolstered by seasonal infiltrations of larger spawners or enterprising wanderers coming up out of Elevenmile. This remarkable section, in the early years of public access, came to be known reverently by many anglers as the "Dream Stream." There were thousands of rainbows per mile, and many of them were in the sixteen- to eighteen-inch class. They could be seen holding in the weed-bottomed currents and feeding rhythmically on abundant populations of tiny mayflies. Sometimes, a half-dozen or more would bunch below the feet of a wading angler, nearly nosing up to his boots, and gobble up the nymphs he kicked loose.

The rainbows are still there, although not in the numbers they once were. Whirling disease has exacted a toll, and stream-deterioration problems have necessitated a stream-improvement project by the Colorado Division of Wildlife. In summer and early fall, a dependable, daily spinner fall of mating Trico mayflies continues to provide two- to three-hour spates of morning dry-fly action, with rising trout inspecting tiny spentwing dry flies presented on cobweb-thin leader tippets. If fly-fishing is a religion, this is morning mass.

But the other twenty-five or so miles of stream that the state acquired above Spinney Mountain and Antero reservoirs at a cost of some $4 million in sportsmen's license money have so far not lived up to their advance billing. The truth is that years of cattle grazing, which caused bank collapse, siltation, and featureless stream bottom, coupled with erratic flows from dams, crippled what once was very good trout habitat. In some stretches, overfishing by clubs or lease groups played a part. The recovery will be a long, tedious, expensive one, but state authorities have begun the process with some stream-improvement work and conservative regulations.

The real lore of Colorado's South Platte River was cultivated in the four-mile section of Cheesman Canyon and in the fifteen miles or so of water from the private Wigwam Club (at the mouth of the canyon) down through Deckers, Trumbull, and on to Long Scraggy Peak and Twin Cedars. The upper canyon is a kind of wilderness retreat for anglers who make the mile walk on a winding trail to reach the roadless part of the canyon.

Through drought, flood, deep-freeze winters, wildly fluctuating flows out of Cheesman Dam, the intense pressure of visiting anglers from Denver, Colorado Springs, and other points, the threat of yet another huge dam and reservoir, and now the ravages of whirling disease, the South Platte trout in and below Cheesman Canyon have periodically suffered—but they have endured.

Even in the old days of an eight-trout limit and bait fishing, the river's generous storehouse of browns and rainbows—up to 5,000 per mile—somehow withstood the onslaught. Given conducive spring and fall flows, the trout spawned successfully. The browns are more consistent survivors than the rainbows, but over the decades, a wild, South Platte rainbow evolved that many think is a distinct subspecies all its own. Numbers of rainbow trout have been reduced by as much as 75 percent in some sections by the effects of the whirling-disease parasite, but there is hope that supplemental stocking of fingerlings and a gradually evolving trout resistance to the parasite eventually will prevail.

The method police are always with us, standing ready and more than willing to instruct us all on the precise techniques by which it is proper to catch a trout with fly tackle. To the method police, anything short of a dry fly is a compromise at best and an outrage at worst, although shallow-fished wet flies and streamers are okay if absolutely necessary—not the ultimate, but okay. Dead-drift nymphing with weighted flies or weighted leaders is an abomination unto the lords of angling.

What strikes me as askew about this way of thinking is not the conviction that dry-fly fishing epitomizes the ultimate grace and visual beauty of hooking a fish on flies. I agree with that. Nor am I bothered by the fact that some of us are willing to catch fewer fish, or no fish, in order to use the fly-fishing approach that pleases us the most when we do catch one. After all, we fish because it gives us pleasure, and each angler is the arbiter of the parameters that form the pleasure. What troubles me is the subjective judgment that anything less than the aesthetic ultimate—however much skill the "lesser" technique requires—is somehow tainted. That sort of thinking, it seems to me, is the bridge that takes us across the river into the swamp of superciliousness. I see nothing crude or threatening in the judicious, skillful application of nymph-fishing tactics.

The modern history and evolution of fly-fishing on the South Platte do not enthrall the method police, because this history is grounded largely in the dead-drift, floating-line, weighted-leader, strike-indicator method of nymphing. I know that it wasn't invented on the South Platte, but I'm sure it was refined there and later on the Roaring Fork.

Whatever else you may say or think about floating-line, dead-drift nymphing, you can't say it doesn't work. It works with incredible efficiency in the hands of an expert. And much of today's expertise had its roots in the runs, pools, and pocket water of the South Platte. In fact, the refined nymphing techniques developed on the Platte were a natural extension of the personality of the fishery. The trout subsist primarily on minutiae—tiny midges and mayflies—and the cold releases from Cheesman Dam render sporadic, highly seasonal hatches of adult insects. Therefore, most of the time, you match the minutiae that's *under* the surface, not on it—often, there isn't anything *on* the surface.

I got my first lesson in the South Platte nymphing method (in my mind, the addition of a strike indicator is what distinguishes it from the Roaring Fork method) about thirty years ago. For the first few years that I fished the river, in my mind the season didn't start until spring runoff subsided. It ended with the first snows of November, and it revolved around dry-fly hatch matching. Then it dawned on me that all these trout really didn't disappear in winter, or in the early spring prior to runoff. (Nor did they stop feeding during periods when no insects were hatching.) In fact, it was obvious from the first few times I visited the river in March and April that, if anything, the trout were easier to find because they weren't scattered. The water was low and clear, and the survival imperatives of trout in extremely cold winter currents meant that they were bunched up in unbelievable concentrations in the gentler, deeper flows. But I couldn't catch them—not even with the few standard nymph patterns I had in my arsenal.

The watershed day for me came one bright afternoon in April as I was driving up the river road near Trumbull, staring wistfully out the windows of the vehicle at the inviting, fish-filled runs beside the road. I had fished a couple of runs to no avail and was looking for new water, as if my problem was as simple as finding a magic spot. Few people were fishing, although the warmth of the sun made the air temperature feel much more comfortable than the forty-five or so degrees it actually was. Just then, I looked to my right at the river, where a sweeping bend pressed in against the embankment of the road, and I saw a man standing at the tail end of the run. He was facing upstream, he had a fly rod in his hands, and the rod was bent to the struggle of a trout.

I came to a stop at a pullout, got out, and walked over to watch. The wader-clad angler was using a bamboo rod equipped with an old Hardy reel. He deftly levered the trout into the shallows, carefully removed the hook, looked at the fourteen-inch brown appreciatively, and released it.

"How you doing?" I said by way of introduction.

"Not bad," he said. "You?"

"Not good," I said. "At least not with the trout."

He clucked sympathetically, then waded back to his original position and paused a moment, as if trying to decide whether to resume casting in the presence of this intrusive stranger. He may have been thinking that it was his bad luck to be landing a trout when some ya-hoo happened along to horn in on the action. But I had left my rod and vest in the car and apparently I looked harmless enough, because he stripped out line, false cast a couple of times, then shot a cast almost straight upstream. About three seconds and five feet of drift later, he was into another trout.

I was flabbergasted. This guy seemed to be making a mockery of my own efforts earlier. When he had landed yet a third brown and released it, I decided to pull out all the interrogatory stops. Normally, I feel uncomfortable asking probing questions about how somebody else is catching fish, but I was now the outdoor editor of a major daily newspaper, and after all, it was my *job* to ask, right? So I told him who I was and waited for his reaction to the bottom-line question: "What are you using?"

Whether out of some sense of public service or the subtle urgings of flattered ego, Bill Howard, who, I learned shortly, was a Denver-area restaurant manager and a South Platte veteran, opened up and explained it to me. He held the nymph that he said he was using between his thumb and index finger. What I saw gleaming back at me looked at first glance like somebody's disjarred gold-tooth filling.

"What," I asked, "is that?"

"Brassie," he said, grinning. "South Platte Brassie."

It occurred to me that this guy might be setting me up for some sort of practical joke, but the little copper-wire-wound hook, glittering goldlike in the glare of the sun, was still attached to his leader tippet. And I had just seen him hook three trout on it, in successive casts.

"How many trout have you caught?" I stammered.

"I think that last one was about fourteen or fifteen, but I lost count a little while ago."

The copper-wire nymph was just part of the revelation. The second part was a small, cylindrical, fluorescent-red-painted cork about five feet up on the leader above the fly. Between the cork—held in place by a toothpick inserted in its hollow stem—and the copper "fly" was a half-inch-long strip of twisted-on, ribbon lead.

The cork, Howard explained, was his strike indicator. It was a rough-cut predecessor of what has become a wide range of strike indicators now in common use—everything from fluorescent-dyed leader butts to tufts of macrame yarn. A floating indicator on the tricky currents of moss-bottomed streams such as the South Platte serves not only as an easily visible tip-off to a strike, but a way to drift tiny weighted nymphs without current drag or bottom hang-ups.

From that day forward, I caught trout—many of them—on Brassies from size 16 to 22, and I was to learn that another Platte veteran, Gene Lynch of Colorado Springs, was the acknowledged innovator of the pattern. It eventually became a standard item in the nymph boxes of many American fly-fishermen. (Nymph patterns wound or ribbed with copper wire, of course, were not pioneered on the Platte. English experts such as Frank Sawyer were using variations of them long before the birth of the South Platte Brassie.)

After I met him and had the privilege of occasionally fishing with him, Lynch told me how he chanced to discover the remarkable utility of an all-copper nymph. Seems he was tying some nymphs one day and was weighting the shanks with fine copper wire. He was interrupted in his labors after winding one of the small hooks. Not having time to finish the fly with dubbed fur, as he intended, he tossed the glittering wire-wound hook into a fly box and forgot about it. Later, out on the river, he was nymph fishing and realized after hanging up and having to re-rig that he had run out of lead split shot to attach above the fly. In a flash of improvisation, he spied the copper-wound hook in his fly box and decided to tie it in as added weight above the fur-bodied nymph he was using. In short order, he was hooked up with a seventeen-inch rainbow, and when he landed it, he discovered to his amazement that the trout had glommed onto—not the bottom nymph—but the "unfinished" copper-wound hook. Two sizable trout later, both duped by the new "fly," Lynch realized that all this was more than just a fluke.

Thus was born the South Platte Brassie.

For a long time, I wondered what the hell the trout could think this thing resembled, and I speculated about sparkling gravel caddis cases, orange-colored scuds, and various other possibilities. Finally, it dawned on me that in smaller sizes, the Brassie, when tied with nothing more complicated than the copper wire and black tying-thread head, was a simple replica of a bright-colored midge larva.

I wrote a column about the Brassie shortly after that fateful encounter with Bill Howard, and Jim Poor's shop was suddenly flooded with requests for the pattern. A few weeks later, I asked a skeptical Poor—who looked upon nymph fishing as a last resort in the fly-fishing scheme of things—what he thought the trout took the Brassie to be. Asking him about a copper nymph was like asking Pavarotti what he thought about Pearl Jam.

"I think," he said, grinning sardonically, "they take it for a Mepps spinner."

It was enough for me to know that they took it.

The cycle continues: The selective trout of the South Platte educate the anglers, and the anglers educate fellow anglers. Jim Poor, Bill Howard, and Gene Lynch were among those who educated me—who taught me the South Platte system and the ways of the trout. There were and are many others who have made their marks on the Platte—men who honed their fly-fishing skills there and came to be identified with the river. Among them are Tuck Squier, Ralph Smith, Bill Shappell, Joe Butler Jr., Bob Good, Ed Marsh, A. K. Best, John Gierach, Roger Hill, Chuck Jenkins, Koke Winter, Des Yorgin, Rim Chung, Charlie Meyers, Bill Logan, Bill Phillipson, Dick Mill, Scott Ratcliff, George Uyeno, Pat Dorsey, and Randy Smith. Some of them are no longer with us. They no longer wade the river and cast to finicky risers in silken currents, except in the memories of those who knew them and fished with them. But they are forever linked in my mind with the South Platte.

Along with the men are the fly patterns that are unique to the river. The South Platte, to me, has always been the River of Oddball Flies, like the Brassie. Another is the Miracle Nymph, a name that belies the pattern's simplicity. All it amounts to is a small hook wound with bright white floss and ribbed with fine gold wire. It, too, is basically a midge larva pattern, or, if adorned with a wing protrusion on the top side, a midge pupa or emerger.

Still another is the Buckskin Nymph, or Chamois Skin. Also a paragon of simplicity, it incorporates a larvalike body of wound strips of either light-colored deerskin or chamois (the material historically used to wash cars). It usually includes a short, sparse tail of brown feather fibers and sometimes a beard tied in at the throat of the fly. It was introduced to me by the late Jim Van Meter, a Colorado flytier who constructed it with chamois strips in relatively large hook sizes (14 and 16). I found it to be very effective on the Platte, particularly during cloudy periods or in the low-light conditions of early and late in the day. I believe the Platte trout took it to be a crane-fly larva, but in the smaller sizes, it served as a midge or scud imitation.

Aside from the Brassie, the most important contribution to the fly boxes of American anglers to come from South Platte lore is the RS-2—an all-purpose nymph pattern that, depending on size, can resemble the aquatic stages of a midge, a mayfly, or even a caddis. RS-2 stands for "Rim's Semblance, Style 2." It was born in the tying vice of Rim Chung of Denver, a self-taught fly-fisherman who began as a frustrated spin-fisherman.

When Chung came to Colorado from Seoul, South Korea, in 1968, he had a strong desire to catch Colorado trout but only the weakest clues on how to go about it. He began to fish with spinning tackle but rarely caught anything when he encountered the selective trout of the Platte and other waters. Two years later, he was ready to give up. Then a friend suggested he take up fly-fishing. "What the hell is fly-fishing?" Chung asked his friend. Chung then began to fish with dry flies, but it was still frustratingly unproductive or, at best, inconsistent. Finally, he met someone who offered to take him nymph fishing. "What the hell is nymph fishing?" Chung asked.

His progression to becoming a successful trout fisherman was fairly swift after that. Chung developed his nymphing skills and learned to tie flies. He decided to try to develop a nymph pattern that was a general suggestion—a semblance— of almost any hatching aquatic insect, depending on size. What emerged was a pattern that is constructed with a Tiemco 101 hook that has a straight eye, in sizes as big as 14 and as small as 24. Two strands of microfibers or beaver guard hairs constitute a widely split tail. The body, or abdomen, is slenderly dubbed beaver fur, either natural gray or dyed black, olive, or some other color. A thicker thorax section is also dubbed beaver fur. The almost directly upright short wing is tied between the thorax and the abdomen on the top side and consists of a clump of gray, webbed saddle hackle fibers, or CDC material, trimmed with scissors into a triangular shape.

Today, the fame of the RS-2 has spread far beyond the South Platte, but it stands as testimony to the ingenuity of the anglers who honed their skills on its challenging currents. I count myself fortunate to be part of the history of such a river.

CHAPTER 4
HAIL TO
THE CHIEF

AS A MATTER OF GENERAL POLICY, I VIEW WASHINGTON BUREAU-
cracies with the same degree of trust I would offer a stranger
who wanted to sell me a gold watch on a downtown Denver
street corner. But there will always be a warm spot in my
heart for the Environmental Protection Agency (EPA) and
former President George Bush for a solitary, simple reason:
The EPA, during Bush's administration, put a stop to an abomination called Two Forks Dam.

What a fisherman, or anyone who values natural resources, must understand is that dams giveth and dams
taketh away. In the balancing equation of river sections and
impoundments between those sections, black and white
blend into shades of gray. Some of our greater trout fisheries
are now found in tailwater sections, where the stabilizing in-
fluences of dams guarantee predictable conditions for the basics of trout survival—food, hospitable flows and water
temperatures, and spawning territory. On the other side of the
equation, reservoirs have wiped out some of the finer river
fisheries and riparian corridors—rivers that were wild and
free-flowing and home to trout, bass, or other species that
didn't need a helping hand from the hatchery. Two Forks
Reservoir would have destroyed the most vital twenty miles
of the main-stem South Platte River near Deckers, along with
several additional miles on the North Fork.

Beyond the presence of trout, South Platte Canyon is a
unique environment. Ponderosa pines and granite ridges stand
sentinel over green currents flowing in alternating pools, runs,
and riffles. Eagles soar on canyon updrafts, mallards nest in

the side channels or paddle contentedly behind beaver dams, and mule deer appear in the morning mist to get a drink of water. Hundreds of thousands of recreational visitors, of which anglers are just a part, visit this natural wonderland each year.

Two Forks Dam would have given us another motorboat lake, and not a very good one for fishing purposes at that. It would have been steep sided and deep and conducive more to trolling for kokanee salmon or lake trout than fly-fishing for rainbows or browns. It would have been a fluctuating bathtub of a reservoir, drained at times to satisfy the thirsts of a rapidly growing metropolitan area surrounding what we like to call the Mile High City. Two Forks would have guaranteed the quick burgeoning of an already sprawling suburbia from as far north as Boulder to as far south as Colorado Springs, with the Denver area at the hub. Presto—the Piled High City. It is happening anyway to a degree, but Two Forks would have accelerated the process and heaped the pile even higher than it will eventually turn out to be.

Thousands of people who valued the river for different reasons, depending on their relationship to it, fought Two Forks tooth and nail. Some fought it because they were trout fishermen. Some fought it because they were "environmentalists," a label that is sometimes difficult to define and not necessarily as stodgy as it sounds. Some fought it because they opposed growth along the Front Range, and to them this was just another enabling action to foster that growth. Some fought it because they lived along the river.

Trout Unlimited and an environmental coalition fought the project, sitting down with the "water buffaloes"—as the water-development proponents came to be contemptuously labeled by some of us—to try to work out alternatives. It eventually became clear that in the minds of the Two Forks proponents, there were no alternatives—not even water-conservation measures by the existing users themselves. If the people desired bluegrass lawns in the western desert, then, by God, they should have them. This is, after all, a nation that dutifully, and at some cost, plants, cultivates, and harvests lawn grass.

So the EPA stepped in when the Army Corps of Engineers said that it would issue a construction permit to the Denver Water Department and its suburban water-provider allies. George Bush, an angler of sorts himself, had declared (amid much derisive skepticism) that he wanted to be the "environmental president," and he had a man in place at the reins of EPA—William Reilly—who would help him do that. In 1989, EPA vetoed the proposed dam, saying that the would-be dam builders had failed to pursue the practical water-storage and conservation alternatives to Two Forks that would prevent the environmental destruction of a canyon river.

The any-development-is-good-development types, the Chamber of Commerce geeks, the ones who believe that bigger is always better, no matter how good things are now— screamed like impaled pigs. How could we build a New York–size Denver if we couldn't give all these new folks a drink of water? How could we fortify the tax base?

This is the mentality that believes if you have a delightful and intimate party consisting of a dozen people, it will be all that much more of a blast if you go out and scare up two or three dozen others to bring the merriment up to the level of bedlam.

One of the stock arguments against saving South Platte Canyon was that it was a heavily used, trashed-out recreational area, not a pristine wilderness. Of course it isn't a pristine wilderness. That's what makes it so much more valuable—it is near to its users and serves the outdoor recreational needs of millions of city and town dwellers. If only a few hardy hikers and horseback riders got to see it, it would be worth much less. As it turned out, Pike National Forest officials and others did a pretty good job of cleaning up the riverbanks and regulating parking and other recreational pressures. The river has been nominated for official wild and scenic status, which would slam the door on any further dam construction.

Many of us fought the Two Forks project for twenty years or more—anglers, writers, environmentalists, and conservation organizations such as Trout Unlimited. To me, the South

Platte was the nursery that nurtured my growing and enduring love for trout fishing. I wrote my first newspaper column opposing Two Forks Dam in 1971. It was to be the first of many.

I remember a fine spring day, back before the EPA veto, when my two young sons, not even in high school yet, accompanied me on a day of fishing on the Platte. As we drove back along the river road in the half-light of dusk, we passed under the shadow of the imposing, jagged ridge known as Long Scraggy Peak, where mountain lions still made their dens. We also passed roadside signs posted by the scattered residents of the area, people who lived in the cabins and frame houses up on the ridges along the lower river. These folks stood to lose not just a river, but their homes. "Entering Endangered Area," the signs advised, and "All This Will Be Under 350 Feet of Water." "Recreation—Not Wreck Creation."

My younger son asked about the lake that would be formed. "Will there be trout in the lake?" he inquired.

How, I wondered then, do you explain to a twelve-year-old the difference between wild, river-sleek trout that rise to a fly and the pale, nonspawning fish that would be stocked in a reservoir fished by trollers rigged with dangling flasher blades and nightcrawlers? How do you define, for him, the pull of a home river on an angler's life and soul?

"Yes," I said finally, "there will be trout and people will fish for them."

The older sibling spoke after a brief silence. "But it won't be the same, will it?" he said.

No, I thought, it could never be the same.

Today, my sons and daughter, and tomorrow, their children, can still come to a river to fish or just to look and admire. They can live their big-city lives knowing that the natural wonder of a canyon river is still there, just out of sight beyond the purple-gray silhouettes of the nearest mountains—a tenacious fighter still bobbing and weaving successfully against the wild roundhouse rights of unbridled development.

Thank you, George Bush.

THE RICHNESS OF rivers

PART TWO

CHAPTER 5

Laramie Legacy

SOME RIVERS AND INSECT HATCHES ARE INEXTRICABLY INTER-
twined, sort of like a devoted couple in a long, strong marriage. The Henry's Fork and the Green Drake mayfly come to
mind; the Madison and the salmonfly; Silver Creek and the
Trico; Colorado's Arkansas River and the caddis; the San Juan
and the midge; and the giant *Hexagenia* mayfly, or "Michigan
caddis," of the Au Sable and other rivers in northern Michigan.

There are innumerable, less-famous streams all across the
country with their own hallmark hatches—streams that are
seldom ballyhooed outside the relatively near environs of the
streams themselves. Some of these hatches last only a few
weeks and some only a matter of days. But their arrival is an-
ticipated by local fly-fishermen with the happy eagerness of
children counting the days until Christmas or summer vacation from school. Often, these hatches herald the first serious
dry-fly fishing of the season.

It is with just such anticipation that many fishermen in
Colorado and Wyoming annually awaited the onset of what
long ago became known as the Quill Gordon Hatch on the Big
Laramie River in southern Wyoming and northern Colorado.

"Big Laramie" is something of a misnomer, and so is the
name for the hatch. Nowhere along its length can the river be
classified as particularly big, at least by the standards of many
trout rivers. In its most productive stretches, the river is no
more than eighty feet wide. A deep run is seldom more than
hip deep. The size of the Big Laramie is further diminished
every summer as irrigators and other water users divert its
flows for various purposes, including the greening of ranch

hay meadows. By August, it is little more than a tepid trickle in its middle reaches.

Flow fluctuations at the critical turning point between the last gasp of spring runoff and the beginning of summer water diversion can be as wild as a drop of one to two feet in a single day. Actually, the only reason for the "big" designation is to distinguish the main river from its chief tributary, which is called, naturally, the Little Laramie.

The river is born in the outflow of Chambers Lake in northern Colorado, not far from the spine of the Continental Divide. It flows northward toward Wyoming, tumbling pale-amber clear and brooklike through high-elevation conifer forests. Then it begins to spread out and take on a richer tea color in the alder- and cottonwood-lined channels through ranch properties on both sides of the Colorado-Wyoming line. The copper color seems fitting—it complements the burnished hues of the river's chief species, the brown trout. The river spreads out onto flat ranchland on the high plains of southern Wyoming before winding again into small canyons and through Wheatland Reservoir before joining the North Platte.

Most of the public access is available near the Colorado-Wyoming line. Soon after it crosses north into Wyoming, the Laramie riffles past the homes and cabins of Woods Landing, Wyoming, and slides under the Woods Landing Bridge, hard by the little community's gas station, post office, bar, restaurant, and small, dilapidated cabins. Nowhere does a western trout stream look more western, nor more picturesque.

Samuel S. Woods, a freight hauler and entrepreneur, founded Woods Landing in 1890. He turned it into what historical footnotes call a "resort," where he and his wife bartered creature comforts and lodging to weary travelers. The visitors sought not much more than the basics of food, rest, and shelter for the night. By the late 1920s, Woods Landing included the rough-hewn cabins along the river and a notched-log community hall that offered Saturday night dances attended by the area's cowboys, lumberjacks, and, eventually, college students from the University of Wyoming at Laramie. By midcentury, the "resort" had become a pocket-size community and summertime visitors to Woods Landing had become mostly fly-fishermen. They began to rent the cabins and buy whisky and beer in the bar and greasy steaks and hamburgers in the cafe. But they cared less about the creature comforts than they did about the creatures of the river itself—brown trout and mayflies, the perfect combination for classic dry-fly fishing.

"Has the Quill Gordon Hatch started yet?" became a predictable question about the end of June in the fly shops in Denver, Boulder, and Fort Collins. The "Greenies"—Colorado vehicles have green license plates, and this is the somewhat derisive term given to Colorado visitors by Wyoming natives—were poised to migrate north. The hatch could generally be counted on to begin by July 1, sometimes earlier, and peak between July 4 and July 10. It seldom lasted more than two weeks, but those two weeks offered dry-fly action that would have brought joyous tears to the eyes of Theodore Gordon, the Catskill-region angling pioneer who is considered the father of American dry-fly fishing and who invented the Quill Gordon pattern.

One of the beauties of the Laramie hatch was that it meant big mayflies and big patterns to match them. Seldom was anything smaller than a No. 12 dry fly needed, and sometimes the right match was a No. 10. By Colorado and southern Wyoming hatch-match standards, this was huge—a Boeing 747 compared to a hang glider.

The major dry-fly action of the day usually commenced about 10 A.M. and lasted for at least three hours. To a dry-fly man who had his act together—whose biorhythms and stars were aligned correctly—this translated into anywhere from half a dozen to two dozen hefty browns caught and released (or a legal limit caught and creeled). The hatch was that most glorious of trout-fishing events—a natural phenomenon pervasive enough to lure the normally reclusive browns out of their brush-and-rock hideaways along the banks to feeding stations in the primary currents in midriver. They were suddenly, wonderfully, out of character, cruising around boldly in the runs and riffles like reckless rainbow trout.

Strangely enough, an upright-wing, dun-style Quill Gordon, or sometimes an Adams or Green Drake, was usually all that was needed to bring strikes from browns going twelve to seventeen inches on the average. For a stream the size of the Laramie, this amounted to a surface-feeding orgy of lunkers.

What was strange about it, I discovered after I had fished the hatch annually for several years, was that the key mayfly in this happy scenario wasn't technically a Quill Gordon but a Western Gray Drake. A friend and I made this determination after we captured a few of the mating-stage spinners and took them back in a film canister for a biologist to examine and identify. He soon relayed the information that the bug was *Siphlonorous occidentalis*, which translates to Western Gray Drake.

The puzzling part is that this mayfly, in its nymphal stage, is a burrowing nymph that crawls out along the bottom toward the bank and emerges on the mud, rocks, or bankside debris—like a crawling stonefly. Thus, there are no Gray Drake duns, or very few, riding the current and drying their wings at emergence time. Rather, the insect crawls out at night or in early morning, hangs around in the streamside foliage for a time, then falls in spent-wing configuration onto the water during its mating ritual. All of which would seem to mean that spent-wing patterns should be necessary to match the hatch.

The browns of the Big Laramie didn't make the distinction, or if they did, it didn't matter to them. That was part of the charm of this seasonal blast of surface feeding—it became not an exercise in precise imitation, but a kind of grand harmony between the rhythms of hungrily rising trout and the casting cadences and presentation skills of the angler. Float the fly or any reasonable facsimile in the right lane with no drag, the trout seemed to be saying, and we'll do the rest. It was truly beautiful—a melding of natural imperatives with angling exigencies.

My memories of days on the Laramie are many and rich—days such as Bill Shappell and I spent, fishing the stretch controlled by the owners of the El Rancho Pequeño cabins, where we lounged in the grass in front of our cabin and waited for the rises to begin, smoking cigars and sipping sweatingly cold cans of beer. This was a rough-cut, western version of the English tradition of not casting until a visibly surface-feeding trout appears. In the evening, when the ripples of the last rise died away in the shadows, Shappell and I would retire to the cabin to sip bourbon, listen to a country-western tune (or sometimes, if we felt especially civilized, a classical symphony) on the radio, and prepare thick steaks over a charcoal grill. If it gets any better than that, I'm not sure I could stand it.

I also recall days on the Honholz Ranch on the Colorado side, where one late morning I hooked a ten-inch brown and began cranking it in. Suddenly, there was a much heavier presence, then a huge bulge and wake in the water. All fly-fishermen hear stories like this, but it actually happened: A hook-jawed male brown at least two feet long had clamped the smaller trout crosswise in his toothy jaws and was stubbornly swimming away with it. The silent tug-of-war continued for at least a minute before the predatory older fish finally released his prize.

Besides the free-rising browns, there were attendant charms to fishing the Woods Landing water—eagles soaring over sagebrush slopes, swallows crisscrossing the river in the twilight, brilliantly colored wild flowers in the hay meadows, and mule deer melting in and out of the willow thickets like tawny ghosts.

Another attraction of more bacchanalian proportions was the streamside bar, which was the obvious spot to retire to at approximately 1:30 P.M., about the time the day's primary rise of trout was over. Surface feeding usually resumed at a lesser level again at about 6 P.M., but there were basically only two things to do in the interim—drink in the bar or take a nap in a cabin. Actually, there was a third option—dredging the bottom with nymphs—but that seemed neither necessary nor proper on this hallowed water during this hallmark hatch.

The bar featured a gallon jar filled with water and a slot cut into the jar's lid. At the bottom of the jar was a submerged, upright shot glass. Customers were invited to take a dime, drop it through the slot, and watch it flutter down through the water toward the shot glass. This gave an entirely new meaning to the phrase "dropping the dime," cop jargon for snitching on someone. If the dime happened to land in the glass, the lucky dime dropper was presented with a free beer. There was usually a small mountain of dimes surrounding the shot glass, lying there like some unsalvaged deep-sea treasure, until the bartender got around to gathering up the spoils. The "dime hatch" was likely to blossom anytime after 2 P.M.

The tradition collided with ingenuity and the principles of physics when a fishing partner of mine discovered that he could pinch a dime between his thumb and forefinger and sort of shoot it down the slot, like a kid firing a shooter in a marble game. This gave the dime a slicing trajectory that was far more likely to land it in the bottom shot glass than a haphazard, fluttering fall. More than a dozen full beer bottles sat on the bar in front of a happy group of wader-clad fly-fishermen when the bartender finally caught on to what was happening and shut off the flow of suds. This had somewhat the same sad finality as the end of the midday mayfly hatch.

I remember an afternoon when Ed Sisty of Denver sat over a beer in one of the wooden booths and explained in professorial detail why his new "flat-bodied nymphs" worked so well when there was no hatch in progress. They also produced, he claimed, even when there was a hatch and trout were feeding on the surface. He tied these concoctions with bodies of dyed raffia or flat dental floss on a wire outrigger affixed to the hook. Viewed from the side, they were indeed flat, which he believed conformed to the shape of the nymphal stage of most mayflies and stoneflies.

Sisty had come to Colorado from New York, where he had been a student of the writings of Edward Hewitt and had become fixated, you might say, on flatness. He even designed a flat-bodied fly rod, which he believed was more powerful than round or hexagonal designs. All I know is that his nymphs worked well on the Laramie and several other rivers, and I always kept a few in my boxes, many years after Sisty died of heart trouble. (I never tried the flat-bodied rod.)

Part of the river's charm were the old log cabins at the Landing. The going rate in the 1970s and 1980s was about ten or fifteen dollars per night—worth every penny of it when you considered that the nearest motel was thirty miles away. These quaint edifices were appealingly rustic, especially if you had an appreciation for ambience such as whining mosquitoes finding their way through dilapidated screens, lumpy, sagging mattresses in the configuration of hammocks, and spiders hanging out in the bathroom sink. What made all this bearable—yes, even charming—was the murmuring sound of the river just in back of the cabins. If an aging angler lost the spring in his legs during a day of hard wading, he could regain it on a Saturday night by dropping in on one of the community-hall dances—the plank floor of the dance hall was built, for some reason, on railroad boxcar springs. As one regular described it, "When you dance, the floor comes up to meet you."

The trout came up to meet you, too. There were times when the Big Laramie browns gulped a No. 10 Quill Gordon, times when they took a No. 12 Adams, times when they slashed into a No. 14 Letort Hopper (no doubt taken for a caddis fly, which also hatched sporadically during the mayfly period), times, usually in the morning prior to the hatch, when they attacked a large nymph fished close to the bank, and times when a soft-hackled emerger fished across and downstream worked when a dry fly didn't.

All of this posed something of a question as to why trout-feeding behavior could vary so much during one predominant hatch, until I happened to talk to George Baxter, a Wyoming resident who for many years was a biology professor at the University of Wyoming in Laramie. Baxter was both a scientist and a fly-fisherman, and he brought studious attention to the seemingly contradictory nature of the feeding patterns of the Big Laramie browns.

For one thing, he noted, there was more than one hatch of mayflies on the Laramie during the key late-June to mid-July period. (After mid-July, the river dropped so low from diversions that the browns reverted to their reclusive ways, and hatches to entice them out of it were irregular and mostly insignificant.) In addition to the *Siphlonurus* (Gray Drake) hatch, there were periodic emergences of *Drunella grandis* (the Western Green Drake), *Ephemerella inermis* and *Ephemerella infrequens* (Pale Morning Duns), and *Rithrogena robusta* (Red Quill) mayflies. This sort of indicated that anything generally imitative of the size, color, and behavior of any of those insects was likely to be accepted by an aggressively feeding brown trout. The acceptance of dun patterns during what would seem to be a period of spent-wing activity would indicate more than one mayfly hatching. The periodic success of wet-fly patterns fished across and down would conform to midday emergences of PMDs, Green Drakes, or Red Quills.

Of course, I'm not dead solid certain about any of this, and during most of the time I spent on delightful summer days on the Big Laramie, I didn't care whether I had it entomologically precise or not. Recreational pleasure shouldn't require scientific equations to verify its value. I get no particular charge out of talking or thinking in Latin. I just knew that it all came together in a magical sort of symmetry.

You may wonder why, other than the fact that I view all of this through the hazy lens of memory, I'm describing all of it in the past tense. The river is still there, its flows not changed substantially over decades. It did not fall victim to dams or channelization. But the Quill Gordon hatch, the Gray Drake hatch, or whatever you choose to call it, isn't what it used to be on the Big Laramie. There are indications that the brown-trout population isn't what it used to be, either. In recent years, catching the hatch just right has become a crap shoot with loaded dice. The bugs may or may not be there, and they are never there now in the profusion they used to be. The water is often too high, cold, and murky or too low and warm, although those were problems that occasionally had to be dealt with even in the "good old days."

The main theory of many Big Laramie old-timers is that increased county-agency insecticide spraying of mosquitoes along the river, which often coincided with the onset of the mayfly hatch, not only did a number on the mosquitoes but on the mayflies as well. I don't doubt it, although I have no way to prove it. But to a fly-fisherman, a mosquito-free day and evening is a poor swap for a riseless river. I suspect that there has been a bit more to it than that, including drastic fluctuations in the water level in late spring and summer, creating an imbalance of habitat conditions that took its toll on both trout and aquatic insects over the years. Then there is the inexorable development and varying degrees of pollution that occur along riparian corridors throughout the West.

I suppose that the dance floor at Woods Landing still rises to meet the happy revelers, even if sometimes the trout don't, and that the dimes still flutter down in the bar's gallon jar, if nobody else has caught onto the squirting technique. But old-timers tend to dwell on the old days. That is the way of it, always.

CHAPTER 6
san juan
circus

PAT DORSEY, SITTING HUNCHED OVER A FLY-TYING VICE FASTENED
to the edge of a campground picnic table, suddenly spit out a
few choice words of the four-letter variety. A gust of warm
summer wind had swept through the cottonwood trees and
across the campground, blowing some two dozen No. 26
hooks right out of their small box. Dorsey had been using
them to tie midge-pupa patterns. Just that fast, the hooks
were lost in the gravel under the table, and finding them
would be like tracking down fleas in a pile of compost. Some
minutes later, after tending to a camp chore, I returned to
where Dorsey and Frank Slaninger were still crawling around
under the picnic table.

"Have you found most of the hooks?" I inquired.

"No," Frank said, "but we're training the ants to find them."

One thing you don't have to do on the San Juan River, below Navajo Dam in northwestern New Mexico, is train the
trout to find them. If a minuscule hook is credibly adorned
with something resembling the larval or pupal stages of insects in the *Diptera* order—that is, midges—it has a very
good chance of being rudely requisitioned by a rainbow trout
that will be sixteen to twenty-four inches long.

Strangely enough, this was my first visit to the fly-fishing
circus on the San Juan. I suppose I have this antisocial atti-
tude toward certain fisheries—the more famous and crowded
they get, the less likely I am to spend much time there. It is
said that if you can build a better mousetrap, the mouse-
plagued part of the populace will beat a path to your door.
Certainly, if you can build a dam and create a better trout

stream—or, as in this case, a trout stream that didn't even exist before—the fly-fishing world will burn up the highways to reach it. If you end up with a bunch of trout that fatten themselves on aquatic worms and billions of midges, and you slap regulations on the whole thing to guarantee that those trout will stay in the river, you have in effect erected a national shrine. And who am I not to make occasional pilgrimages?

The San Juan is an aberration as trout rivers go. It flows blue-green, clear, and cold out of the bottom of Navajo Reservoir and slides in a weaving pattern of channels, riffles, and holes through what is essentially desert country. Red sandstone bluffs and ridges dotted with chaparral and juniper provide the backdrop, with willows and cottonwoods framing some of the flats. Where tepid, muddy water once flowed in unpredictable spurts and trickles, reservoir outflows ranging from 500 to 5,000 cubic feet per second are released from the dam. The water temperature is an almost constant and shockingly icy forty-two to forty-four degrees, regardless of the time of year, and anybody wearing lightweight waders, even in summertime, is standing on numb feet within minutes.

The impression that a well-traveled fly-fisherman gets when he first fishes the San Juan is that maybe the Henry's Fork of the Snake River has died and been reincarnated in the desert Southwest. No, the San Juan isn't a huge spring creek running through lush, grassy meadows. But there are remarkable similarities. One is the presence of large, selective rainbow trout. These fish generally disdain popular-in-the-West fly patterns such as the Royal Wulff, Rio Grande King, Elk Hair Caddis, and Muddler Minnow. Another parallel is the presence of crowds of anglers who turn out day after day. There is a sort of "we're all in this together" mentality, which helps in coping with the crowds.

There is also an undercurrent of macho competition going on in the best runs, or maybe that's just my perception. But a lot of the guys you see are among the more skilled fly-fishermen in the West, and if they are hooking trout and you are not, you can't help but wonder at your own inadequacies. Then you try to shake off that feeling, because this isn't meant to be a contest between anglers. It's supposed to be a test between you and the trout—between you and the river. But the competitive overtone can be blocked out of your mind or avoided entirely by fishing some of the more obscure and less-pressured side channels of the river, of which there are many.

The San Juan is the home of the famous—and remarkably effective—San Juan Worm pattern, and of the infamous Texas Hole, which, with its elbow-to-elbow clutter, gave birth to the term "combat fishing." Perhaps in part because of the crowds, the San Juan is a river where, if you don't hook at least an occasional three- to five-pound rainbow, you depart with a tucked tail and a bruised ego.

Some anglers look upon—or down upon, to be precise—the San Juan Worm as a large rip in the moral fiber of American fly-fishing. Regardless of what you think about it, there is no doubt that the thing works, and not just on the San Juan. Most tailwaters have prolific populations of aquatic or "sludge" worms.

There are probably as many stories about the origin of the San Juan Worm as there are variations of the pattern, but the version I embrace is the one told by Abe Chavez, the ebullient owner of Abe's Motel and Fly Shop on the river. He tells it this way: Paul Pacheco, a friend and customer of his who was a school principal in Shiprock, New Mexico, often came into the shop in the late 1960s (the dam was finished in 1962) to purchase red-colored Domino Nymphs, a woven pattern then marketed by Hank Roberts of Colorado. It seemed a strange choice, but the school principal was doing pretty well with it. Then one day he came in and showed Chavez a creation of his own—a peculiarly curved hook wound with red material to look like a worm. "This imitates those red worms the trout are getting fat on," Pacheco said. "Those red worms" were, of course, the aquatic worm variety that found the silt-coated channels of the San Juan to be ideal habitat. Thus, said Chavez, was born the San Juan Worm.

But San Juan regulars have found in more recent years that the worm has turned. While the river's rainbows still gorge at times on aquatic worms, the more prevalent and accepted food item on a day-in, day-out, month-in, month-out basis is the midge. Presumably, it is much harder for a sophisticated, hook-scarred trout to detect a phony larva or pupa in near-microscopic sizes than it is to recognize the fraud in a garish-looking, chenille worm more than an inch long. The trout are not quite so gullible as they were in the early years of the San Juan Worm. Even Chavez, who sells thousands of tiny flies, occasionally has trouble positively identifying the smallest of the midge patterns, which can be black, red, gray, brown, olive, or cream-colored. "Once," he claims, chuckling, "I sold a guy a piece of lint, thinking it was a midge nymph." This seems to say that if what comes out of a fly-tying vice looks like it might have fallen out of somebody's belly button, it probably will fool San Juan trout.

Pattern is one thing; presentation is something else. I had learned on the afternoon of my arrival from Denver that dead-drifting a natural-colored San Juan Worm (tied with loose ul-tra-chenille ends on a No. 12 hook) would produce an occasional hookup with a hefty rainbow. But very occasional, as it turned out. That's when I came to the conclusion—as many of the fly-fishermen around me obviously already had—that midges were the answer. It was hard to ignore the midges, because at about midday, they hatched in numbers sufficient to fly into your mouth if you opened it. Dorsey, Slaninger, George Uyeno, and I began to enjoy slightly more frequent hookups using Pat's No. 26 Black Beauty Midge (af-ter he and the ants finally rounded up the stray hooks). We began fishing them under synthetic-foam strike indicators with increased success, but not with the rate of success being enjoyed by a couple of clients of a guide who was choreo-graphing their efforts in a nearby side channel. After chewing on and swallowing a measure of false pride, I asked the guide, who introduced himself as Brian Klein, what his charges were using.

It was not so much what, but how. They were using two-fly rigs and a strike indicator, but the indicator wasn't cork or foam. It was an inch-long tuft of tan-colored yarn, affixed about six feet above the top fly by simply tightening down a loop in the leader. The top fly was an olive midge emerger or Brassie, size 22, and the bottom was a No. 26 Black Midge with a peacock-herl head—virtually the same pattern Dorsey had tied for us. A single microshot was clamped on above the top fly. As Klein generously explained, the yarn indicator landed softly and floated naturally on the surface, without so much of a hinge effect as with a cork-type indicator. It looked to the trout like a floating leaf or piece of flotsam.

Where his presentation (and that of his clients) differed from ours was that dead-drift was only half the technique. Once the indicator and nymphs drifted downstream of the angler's position, he continued to let them drift with some mending and line feeding, but he also allowed the flies to swing upward toward the surface. In other words, drag was utilized, not avoided, and it simulated the rising movement of midge emergers headed toward the surface. This was August, and the trout were more than willing to chase something that appeared to be hatching—in fact, the movement probably created a more lifelike impression than a perfect dead-drift.

My new yarn indicator began to get sucked under the surface with delightful repetition. The first time it happened, a twenty-inch rainbow rocketed immediately upward and came out in a cartwheel, falling back on the 6X leader that connected the bottom midge to the top one. So long, trout, bottom midge, and bottom leader. Re-rigging with near-invisible leader material and tiny flies is part and parcel of the San Juan midging experience. Bring patience and a magnifying optic that clamps to your Polaroids, unless you have eyes like—well, like ants searching for No. 26 midge hooks.

For his part, Dorsey worked out his own version of the San Juan System—a two-fly rig with yarn indicator but with the top fly consisting of a small, tan San Juan Worm and the bottom a No. 26 Black Beauty Midge. Most of his trout came on the midge, but a fair number also responded to the worm imitation, as if the fact that it was drifting next to a midge was some sort of assurance to the fish that it was real.

The first quarter-mile of river below Navajo Dam is under a catch-and-release rule. The next three and one-half miles are one trout, twenty inches or longer. All of this mileage is under a flies-and-lures only restriction with single, barbless hooks. But you seldom see anybody fishing with lures and you almost never see anyone kill a trout. In other words, the rules are pretty well understood by everyone, including the trout. There are many attractions on the San Juan, but campground fish fries aren't one of them. Nor is solitude. But who expects solitude at a circus?

CHAPTER 7

THe Born-AGain Gunnison

WHEN THEY AREN'T ACTUALLY FISHING, FISHERMEN SOMETIMES amuse themselves by asking frivolous questions, such as, what's the greatest trout stream in the country? The question may not be as esoteric as the one about how many angels can two-step on the head of a pin, but it's almost as difficult to answer with any sort of persuasive assurance. A river that becomes widely accepted as "the greatest" may, by definition, become so cluttered with advocates that it fails to fit the description anymore.

But it's entertaining to entertain the question. You get into all manner of objective and subjective criteria, from public access to trout biomass and average size to insect hatches to the legendary stories that become the lore and history of the river. There was a time when authoritative observers such as Joe Brooks placed the Big Hole River in Montana in nomination. The Big Hole is still a jewel of a trout stream when flows are stable, but few people would seriously argue for it as a national standard-bearer these days. There are those who still believe the Madison River fills the bill, even with the infestation of whirling disease that has devastated the Madison's superb rainbow-trout fishery.

In recent years, however, the tailwater advocates tend to name the Bighorn below Yellowtail Dam, with its incredible average of 7,000 trout per mile in the upper section, many of which average sixteen to eighteen inches in length. (Sometimes it may seem that there are almost as many fishermen per mile.) Others would cast their votes for the Green River below Flaming Gorge Dam or, perhaps on a lesser-mileage basis, the

San Juan below Navajo Dam. Before a combination of negative factors sent it into a tailspin from which it is now apparently recovering, the Henry's Fork of the Snake seized the
hearts and minds of fly-fishermen across the land.

But there was also a time, in the decades prior to 1970,
when Colorado's Gunnison River, with its famed Cooper
Meadows–Sapinero stretch and its June stonefly (locally
called "willow fly") hatch, possibly ranked as the most popular and avidly chronicled trout stream in the West, if not the
country. And maybe therein lies the justification for asking
the somewhat pointless "greatest" question in the first place:
If you're not paying attention, you stand to lose all or significant portions of even the greatest trout rivers in the land. A
major, cherished section of the Gunnison certainly was lost.

Once upon a time, "Are the willow flies out on the Gunnison?" was a question that got repeated annually like a seasonal mantra in countless Colorado tackle shops, bars,
sporting-good stores, and over the telephone wires whenever
spring gave way to summer. Red-sided rainbows rose to slash
into bushy flies cast into the swift runs and cottonwood-lined
side channels of a river that wound its way through ranch
meadows and then carved a precipitous slice through the imposing, shadowy depths of the Black Canyon.

The Gunnison became a disappearing blip on the radar
screen of American angling when the first of the three Curecanti
reservoirs was constructed by the U. S. Bureau of Reclamation
in 1965. Blue Mesa Dam and Reservoir was followed in 1968 by
the smaller Morrow Point Reservoir farther downstream, then
by Crystal Dam and Reservoir, completed in 1978 in the heart of
the Black Canyon itself. The middle reaches of the Gunnison
River perished of drowning. Like others who, vicariously or
through personal experience, had come to embrace the legend
of the Gunnison, I mourned its passing when I moved to Colorado from Texas in 1967—even though I had never fished it. It
was my job in ensuing years to cover all aspects of Colorado
fishing as a newspaper outdoor editor, but I stubbornly refused
to sample the fishing at Blue Mesa Reservoir out of deference to
the memory of the gone but not forgotten Gunnison.

What I was overlooking was the simple biological fact that while dams erase river fisheries, or portions thereof, they can also create them. They produce clear-water flows that are cold enough in summer and warm enough in winter to foster productive trout fisheries—sometimes fantastic trout fisheries—often in stretches of river that formerly were murky, silty, tepid havens for little more than rough fish. Thus it was on the lower Gunnison, where the warm, muddy channels through the Gunnison Gorge (at the lower end of the Black Canyon) were transformed almost overnight into a resurgent cold-water fishery with fast-growing rainbows and browns. The Gunnison had been born again.

Rumors of its resurrection began trickling down to me in Denver in 1980 from residents of the areas around the Western Slope towns of Gunnison and Delta. I mentally filed these reports away as chamber-of-commerce hype, if not outright horseshit, probably generated by local folks trying to re-create, or at least relocate, the tourism bonus that the now-buried river once brought with seasonal dependability. Finally, though, I couldn't ignore the calm, measured tones of a couple of old-timers in Delta who assured me by letter and by telephone that the stories I was hearing were true. LeRoy Stanford and Kenneth Parks were old-school dry-fly and wet-fly practitioners who were catching rainbows and browns in the seventeen-inch class or better on frequent excursions to the lower end of the gorge, just above the confluence of the main stem with the North Fork. Their descriptions of the fishing jibed with what I was hearing from those who were beginning to sample the other end—at East Portal just below Crystal Dam—and the few who were taking the steep hiking trails into the upper gorge and then floating the length of it.

On a hot July day, Leo Schmelz and I joined Parks and Stanford in a four-wheel-drive expedition to a spot above the forks. The rough, circuitous route began with a gravel road at the town of Austin, crossed the river to the south side, and soon became little more than a two-track goat trail gouged out of the limestone, sandstone, and shale of the juniper-dotted benches over the greenish but slightly murky river. Chukar partridge paraded across the road in front of us on their way to the river for a drink, just before the road petered out into a hiking trail leading upstream from the forks. The scene twanged some cord of memory of some other river canyon somewhere. It was awhile before I made the connection. Here, the Gunnison looked not a lot different from the desertlike Deschutes River Canyon on the east slope of Oregon's mountains. The question that remained was whether the resemblance extended to the finned inhabitants of the river.

We hiked upstream a quarter mile and chose spots to begin fishing. Parks and Stanford stuck with their dry flies, Leo went with his favorite trout-fishing method, ultra-light spinning with small lures (a technique to which he brought a studious form of magic), and I was prepared to use any fly-fishing method that might provoke results. I tied a No. 14 caddis dry-fly imitation to my 5X leader tippet, hoping that surface action would be the order of the day.

It was—if you liked eight-inch rainbows. I personally have nothing at all against eight-inch rainbows. I feel about them somewhat the same way Maurice Chevalier felt about little girls, who grew into something more substantial. Thank heaven for little trout; without them there is no future in trout fishing. But after my third junior-leaguer taken on the caddis dry, I wondered if my hosts had snared me with a bit of exaggeration. They seemed to be sober-looking types. Still, neither of them, nor Leo, nor I, had taken a trout larger than ten inches after two hours of fishing.

Pulling a handkerchief from a pocket above my hip boots and wiping my sweating face, I was reminded that the temperature was in the nineties and that the water felt slightly warm. It made sense that bigger trout, if indeed they were here, wouldn't be up at the surface in the slower currents. Where would they be? Where the oxygenated water and the more substantial feed were, obviously. And that meant fast, riffled water with a bed of gravel that might hold stonefly nymphs and other sizable nymph or larval forms.

I rigged with a No. 10 Mono Stonefly nymph that was light brown in color and two strips of twisted-on lead eighteen inches above the fly. The twelve-foot leader would allow the nymph to sink and the end of the floating line would be my strike indicator.

I chose the head of a long run, where the water was choppy and superficially white at its most turbulent end. I made several casts with the eight-foot fly rod. Nothing. I shifted around to get a different drift angle. This time, the nymph sunk more quickly, and when the tip of the light green line had floated across from my wading position, it suddenly jerked backward a good foot.

I set the hook. What reared its beautiful head in a cartwheel out of the fast water was no eight-incher. Thirty yards downstream and almost ten minutes later, I beached a muscular male rainbow with pink stripes down its sides. It had fought harder than any other rainbow I could recall taking from Colorado waters. In fact, it fought so long it had exhausted itself, and I failed to revive it in the shallows. I dressed the fish after measuring it—nineteen and one-half inches long.

Obviously, if there were more trout the size of this one in the new Gunnison, I'd have to land them quicker in order to release them safely. I cut back the leader to a stronger 4X. And there definitely were more trout. The next one was a female rainbow almost exactly the same length as the male. Two more in the seventeen- to twenty-inch class followed in fairly short order. They swam away strongly when I released them. Hail to the new Gunnison!

Actually, I reserved conclusive judgment until the next day, when Leo and I returned by ourselves and took eight more trout, including browns that were fifteen and seventeen inches long and four rainbows that were at least twenty inches long, from a fast run just downstream from the forks. Leo, finally convinced that lures were not the answer on this occasion, switched to a fly rod that I loaned him and joined in the nymphing action. We creeled two trout and released the others, but we measured each one that we landed. And the amazing fact was that the average length of all the mature fish caught in two days (Stanford and Parks had taken three in the seventeen-inch class the evening before on dry flies) was in the neighborhood of nineteen inches. That's a pretty classy neighborhood, anywhere in trout country. The lower Gunnison rainbows were a throwback to their famed ancestors—thick-bodied, small-headed, and in marvelous shape.

I wrote a story, with photos, a few days later for the newspaper. The headline said, "Rejuvenated Gunnison Harbors Some Handsome Trout." A year later (in 1982), a story of mine titled "The Born-Again Gunnison" appeared in the pages of *Sports Afield* magazine. The word was out, and I was the tattletale. But this was one of the occasions in my outdoor writing career when nobody called or wrote to complain of what John Voelker, a.k.a. Robert Traver, once termed "kiss-and-tell" journalism—naming, in print, productive trout water. Kissing and telling about the imposing canyon reaches of the Gunnison Gorge was considerably different from pinpointing the location of a three-acre brook-trout pond in the Upper Peninsula of Michigan, obviously. John Voelker couldn't very well afford to give directions to the small jewels that he cherished in the decades of fishing he enjoyed before he died, but the Gunnison was a different—and important—story.

In fact, I take some measure of satisfaction in knowing that what I and others wrote about the reborn Gunnison helped stave off various plans to dam it and divert it even further. Today, many anglers sample the joys of Gunnison Gorge fishing, often with guided floats through some of the more breathtaking scenery in the West. A June stonefly hatch provides spectacular dry-fly fishing if you hit the conditions right, but the standard tactic for fly-fishermen is casting big streamers or nymphs, such as the Bitch Creek, tight to the rocky edges and walls of the river. On hot summer days, nymphing the fast, oxygenated riffles is still the ticket.

Currently, the Gunnison Gorge water is under flies and lures only, and all rainbow trout must be released. The limit is four browns, only one sixteen inches or longer, with twelve- to sixteen-inch fish protected. The no-kill rule on rainbows is partly a concession to the devastation caused by the spread of whirling disease, which primarily plagues rainbows. The disease, and the periodic spring flooding that wipes out spawning efforts, are two negative biological factors that have reduced to some extent the density of Gunnison Gorge trout. But the river still measures up to its official state designation as a "Gold Medal" water.

As for the mid to upper Gunnison, the former stuff of legends, it began in the 1980s to stage its own comeback in the remaining mileage from the Blue Mesa inlet upstream through the town of Gunnison to Almont, where the Taylor and East rivers join to form the Gunnison. The Colorado Division of Wildlife began to stock wild, Colorado River–strain rainbows, and they were doing well until whirling disease threw a monkey wrench into the biological machinery. There is good fishing, however, for rainbows and brown trout, particularly in the first few miles just above Blue Mesa.

But the big story of the 1980s and 1990s on the upper river is the fall run of kokanee salmon out of Blue Mesa. These miniature, landlocked sockeyes—which is actually what they are—are "imprinted" to return upriver through the Gunnison and then through the lower end of the East to the place they were hatched—the Roaring Judy Fish Hatchery on the East River.

There, returning salmon are captured and stripped of eggs and milt, the eggs are fertilized, and the hatched young fish are distributed to other reservoirs or released to make their downstream journey to Blue Mesa. Three or four years later, they come back as fourteen- to eighteen-inch adults that are beginning to turn from silver to gun-metal gray and red. Hundreds of thousands of fish work their way upriver in September and October. The wildlife division many years ago found itself with raceways full of about-to-die, spawned-out salmon and initiated the annual tradition of giving these fish away by the sacksful to anybody who could produce a fishing license. You can debate how delectable a deteriorating kokanee salmon can be, but each fall, fishermen line up to take advantage of the handout.

The upriver run of kokanees, which fight with the same vigor and flare as their larger cousins up in Alaska, has been the source of much delight and some controversy. The delight accrues primarily to fly-fishermen, who rejected the dogmatic baloney from fishery officials and some fishermen who claimed that spawning kokanees couldn't be taken on a fly or lure. (The same thick-sliced misinformation once was dispensed about sockeyes, for that matter.) The "they-won't-hit" bullshit was distributed liberally by fish managers who used that as one of their two main arguments for allowing fall kokanee snagging seasons on major reservoirs, including Blue Mesa. The other argument was that these fish were going to die anyway; therefore, if the masses weren't allowed to snag them with weighted treble hooks or other brutish devices, they would "go to waste."

But while allowing licensed fishermen to jerk heavy hooks into the backs and sides of salmon still in the reservoir, the state fishery architects decided that fly and lure fishermen, who were catching kokanees in the rivers with genuine sporting tactics, couldn't be allowed to keep any Gunnison or East River kokanees for a fresh-salmon meal. The fear was that not enough salmon would get past the ranks of the fly and lure fishermen to replenish the kokanee supply at the hatchery (never mind that many of them were being taken out of the equation by snaggers at the reservoir before they even had a chance to enter the river).

It didn't seem to occur to the fish managers that all this was a classic non sequitur: On the one hand, they were justifying snagging by saying spawn-run salmon wouldn't take flies or lures; on the other, they were writing regulations to "protect" their hatchery resource from fly and lure fishermen.

Fly-fishermen, who were proving on a regular basis that a competent angler could hook dozens of kokanees in a single day using bright streamers and egg-fly patterns, weren't keeping that many salmon anyway. Before the limit was reduced to zero, the average fly-fisherman either released all his kokanees or kept no more than three or four for a meal.

Such is the wonder of the bureaucratic process.

This is one man's opinion, but I don't think we ought to be out there jerking weighted hooks into the sides of fish, whether they're salmon, trout, bass, carp, or African tree-climbing catfish. Many states have outlawed snagging for a number of reasons, not the least of which is the meat-hog mentality it fosters and the fact that other species who happen to be in the water at the same time are snagged along with the spawning salmon.

But the upshot on the upper Gunnison is that it, like the lower river, has experienced a rebirth of sorts, too. It just happens to be seasonal in nature and involves not trout, but salmon. In these uncertain times, you take what the gods of fish management bequeath you.

CHAPTER 8

THe Fork THaT Roars

THE YOUNG MAN IN THE GRIMY BASEBALL CAP CLUMSILY SPILLED his beer all over the table at which he sat. The few other patrons in the Doc Holliday Bar on Grand Avenue in Glenwood Springs looked with mild irritation in his direction, then turned back with bored expressions to their drinks. Baseball Cap, very much in his cups and apparently taking affront at this general apathy, decided to go all the way and turn his table over with a loud crash. Glasses and bottles clattered across the floor. He must have been a regular, because the female bartender, looking tired and as bored as the customers, came over, asked him to quiet down, and began cleaning up the mess.

Then Baseball Cap spotted Don Murphy and me sitting in our nearby booth, where we were tipping a couple of beers, drinking a whimsical toast to the tubercular gunfighter for whom the bar is named. Although his gunfighting exploits occurred in other places, Holliday's remains are buried on a ridge overlooking the town in a spot not more than two miles from the tavern.

Baseball Cap lurched over and sat down beside Murphy without invitation. We both tensed. Then he looked at Murphy's cap and said, "Is your name Garcia?"

Murphy grinned, and I laughed. Murphy's florid face and jutting Irish jaw don't exactly suggest Hispanic descent.

"No," Don said. "It's a fishing-tackle company."

Baseball Cap's eyes brightened. "Oh, are you guys up here fishing?"

Among some residents of and visitors to Colorado's Roaring Fork River Valley, the common denominator in winter isn't skiing—it's fly-fishing the challenging runs of the river that is born in the alpine reaches of Independence Pass and tumbles down through Aspen, Basalt, and Carbondale to dump into the Colorado River at Glenwood Springs.

"Fishing the Fork, huh?" the drunk said. He called out to the bartender for another round of Budweiser. "I like you guys," he confided.

"I'm glad," Murphy said.

"You know," said Baseball Cap, "I got this fly I tie 'specially for the Fork. It's a helluva nymph. Takes me eight minutes to tie it, though. That's the only trouble with the damn thing. Damn, wish I had one to show you."

We never saw the famous eight-minute nymph, but we ended up with directions to a trailer house on a bluff overlooking the river near Carbondale. "Tell him Rudy sent you. He'll let you fish. Some big trout there," Baseball Cap/Rudy said, winking conspiratorially and staggering off in search of new horizons and unturned tables. This was our lucky night—our table was bolted down.

The next morning, the man at the trailer house said he's never heard of Rudy in the baseball cap. So much for inside information from Doc Holliday patrons. Furthermore, the landowner said, he never allows fishing.

There is not a lot of public access on the Roaring Fork, but there's enough if you know the river and don't mind knocking on doors. The problem in some areas is that there are so many small-property landowners you might have to knock on ten doors just to fish a mile of river. And some of them say no.

No matter. We still had plenty of time to kill on this February morning—time it would take for the overnight accumulation of floating slivers and chunks of ice in the river to dissolve in the warmth of a winter sun that was shining blindingly out of a blue sky. It probably would be 10 or 11 A.M. before the fish stirred enough to accept a dead-drifted nymph. The Roaring Fork above Carbondale is partly influenced by the warmer contribution of the Frying Pan flows coming from Ruedi Dam. Warm springs also help. But there is no dam on the Roaring Fork, which makes it almost unique among major Colorado trout streams.

Maybe this was a day for discovery—of new water. Certainly, the Roaring Fork Valley has a history of discovery. Before the coming of the white man, the Ute Indians discovered the medicinal qualities of the hot mineral springs that gushed forth near the confluence of the Colorado (then known as the Grand River) and the Roaring Fork. In 1879, prospectors who journeyed over the pass from Leadville discovered the silver that was to create the small mining boom town of Aspen. In the 1890s, the rest of the state and other parts of the country discovered the therapeutic attractions of Glenwood Springs as a health spa. The warm swimming pool at the Hot Springs Lodge, right by the banks of the Colorado River, is often full on even the colder days. And in the 1940s, a few enterprising, visionary men discovered and began to develop the tremendous skiing potential of Aspen's Ajax Mountain. It marked the reincarnation of Aspen, the burned-out mining town, as a world-class ski mecca and playground of the rich and famous. The average house in Aspen now sells for about $1.5 million (that includes frame bungalows).

It is not officially recorded when fishermen discovered that the Roaring Fork and Frying Pan rivers could be just as productive for fly-fishermen in winter as in the warmer months of the year, but it had to be sometime after 1962. That's the year the Colorado Wildlife Commission authorized a year-round trout season, and anglers no longer had to wait for the opening-day rush in the spring.

Talking it over on the way up Colorado Highway 82, staring down at the inviting river coursing like a blue vein in a body of pure white snow, we decided to postpone further discovery until another day and go instead with familiarity. "Let's try the KOA hole first," I suggested.

So named for the fairly close proximity of a campground and trailer park, the deep KOA run is classic winter holding water for trout and mountain whitefish. It gets pounded hard by fishermen because it abuts a road, but the fish are always there. They don't always respond.

They did respond, however, on this steadily warming morning, although it looked doubtful at first. The air temperature was struggling up from a low of fifteen degrees to what would eventually be forty-four degrees, but it takes only about three degrees of rise in water temperature to make the difference between feeding fish and dead water.

My floating fly line carried down from the lower part of the upper riffle, with the fifteen-foot, 5X-tippet leader, the two strips of twisted-on lead, and the No. 10 flat-monofilament-bodied, brown stonefly nymph sinking below it. (This is a painstaking tie that I concocted myself—my own version of the eight-minute nymph.) I mended the line upstream, knowing that the slightest drag, even though unnoticeable to me, would be met with refusals. When the end of the line, greased earlier to keep it floating high, reached a point straight across from me and just out from the far, undercut bank, it hesitated ever so slightly. I came up on the rod. Somewhere down in the four-foot-deep run, a solid, head-shaking resistance was telegraphed up into the graphite.

This was a rainbow, and it did its best to act like one. It came up in what would have been a jump if the water had been warmer. Instead, it rolled clumsily and dove again, chugging downstream at medium speed. The fight was sluggish, but that would change with the other fish we would hook before our KOA camp-out was over. I released the rainbow and, two casts and drifts later, was into another rainbow.

Fishing the tail-out water below me, Murphy set the hook into his own fish. This one bolted and ran strongly, and I knew what it was—a whitefish. They fight less spectacularly than trout but sometimes a lot more powerfully when the water is very cold. Don's whitefish was a big one—almost eighteen inches long—not uncommon for the Roaring Fork.

The Fork is a river of lunkers when it comes to whitefish. There are world-record-class whitefish in its heavy currents, which means fish of more than five pounds. In fact, for years the listed state record for the species—from the Roaring Fork—corresponded in weight to the world record, taken in Canada. This Roaring Fork specimen was undoubtedly a very big whitefish, but there is some question whether it may have had a pound of buckshot stuffed down its throat.

In the next two hours, before moving to another stretch of river, we hooked and either landed or lost an almost even balance of rainbows and whitefish—enough of both so that this day ranked as a special one on the KOA run. But evidence of the pressure it withstands came in the form of a humorous incident. Having landed a sixteen-inch rainbow, I held it in the shallows and extracted the stonefly nymph from the corner of its jaw. The trout darted away toward the darker green of the deeper water, and I stood up to gather the rod and line for another cast. The rod suddenly jerked downward against a strong pull. Good Lord, I thought, have I hooked a trout without making a cast?

Not exactly. When the rainbow came in easily, as if it were already tired, I examined it and realized that it was the same fish. My nymph was still stuck in the corner of the trout's mouth on the side opposite the one where the first nymph had been lodged. What I had done was remove a nymph that looked like mine—one that had been trailing a length of light leader tippet. Since I hadn't broken off a fly in a fish so far, I knew that the first fly wasn't mine.

In my earlier years of winter fishing in Colorado, I used to refer to winter days on the Roaring Fork and Frying Pan as the "solitude season." You are still not likely to fight elbow-to-elbow crowds (except on the upper Frying Pan below the dam), but the Roaring Fork Valley has become a hodgepodge sea of condos, houses, golf courses, and other development, and winter nymph fishing is no longer a new or arcane art. It remains, however, very rewarding, in part because of no-kill and low-kill regulations, depending on where you are on the Roaring Fork. It is still fine fishing, even if you have to release a fish twice.

This business of lunker whitefish in the Roaring Fork deserves some examination. Once, a state-division-of-wildlife electro-shocking crew took inventory on the Roaring Fork between Carbondale and Basalt and found an astounding 7,000 fish per mile of stream in some spots. That was the good news. The bad news, if you prefer trout, was that about 75 percent of them were whitefish.

It was not always thus. This is not information that is proudly publicized by the state fishery authorities, but there is evidence that no whitefish existed in the Roaring Fork River until the 1960s, after biologists for the Colorado Division of Wildlife decided it might be a neat thing to expand the fishing opportunity on the Roaring Fork. Whitefish are native to the Yampa River drainage and a few other streams north of the Roaring Fork in the northwestern quadrant of Colorado, including the Elk River, the White River, and the Little Snake River. They were even considered something of a winter attraction on the White, where the cold-foot clan generally caught them by drifting live stonefly nymphs captured in seinelike nets.

But there is a natural, historic demarcation line that defines the limits of whitefish habitat, and to this day, they are not found in southwestern Colorado waters such as the Gunnison, the Taylor, the Rio Grande, or the Dolores. Go fifty miles south of the Roaring Fork and you won't find a whitefish. They were once fairly abundant in the upper end of one Eastern Slope stream, the Cache la Poudre, established there by stocking. But no other Colorado streams on the eastern side of the Continental Divide hold whitefish, and indications now are that they are gone, or about gone, from the Poudre.

Perhaps hoping to duplicate the Poudre experiment, a wildlife-division crew gathered up some whitefish from the Yampa and trucked them over to the Roaring Fork. By the mid-1960s, they were starting to turn up with their pursed-lip mouths clamped around flies, lures, and bait, and by the early 1970s, they were generally easier to catch in the Roaring Fork than rainbow or brown trout. They reproduced like rabbits, and during spawning time they clogged the small tributaries of the Roaring Fork and the lower Colorado all the way upstream to Glenwood Canyon. Some anglers curse them, others tolerate them, and still others enjoy fishing for them on purpose. I tend to view them as a pleasant diversion when nothing much else is going on. They are sure as hell willing, almost any time, and that is a quality that should be admired in a game fish.

The angler who first taught me how to catch Roaring Fork whitefish on purpose happened to be a Pitkin County sheriff's deputy. He knew all the whitefish holes between Carbondale and Aspen and was perfectly content to catch whitefish and not trout. As it turned out, he was in charge of guarding Ted Bundy the day the vicious serial killer escaped from an Aspen courthouse building. Bundy proved much more elusive than a lunker whitefish.

Mountain whitefish always bring to my mind the old joke told in southwestern Montana:

"You know why whitefish do so well in the Madison and the Yellowstone?"

"No, why?"

"Because the game and fish department never tried to help them."

Now we know, in Colorado, how well they can do when they get some help.

A veteran guide in Montana once told me, "When I see an out-of-state fisherman who really knows how to nymph fish, he's usually from Colorado." In fact, in some parts of this country, the floating-line, dead-drift, weighted-leader method of nymph fishing is often referred to as "the Colorado method." Author Lefty Kreh calls it the "outrigger method," a reference to the profile of a fisherman standing with reached rod held high, line drooping slightly, as the fisherman short-lines a dead-drifted nymph. Both terms more or less were coined, or at least made famous, on the Roaring Fork River. And the angler who championed the method—who came to be known as the guru of greased-line nymphing (as opposed to sink-tip or sinking-line nymphing)—was Charles Robert "Chuck" Fothergill.

Despite a quiet, almost laconic demeanor, Chuck Fothergill was perhaps Colorado's most famous fisherman. For almost thirty years, he fished, guided, ran a fly shop, tied flies, and wrote guidebooks about fly-fishing in the western states. And much of this activity centered around his beloved Roaring Fork. He was a strong advocate of catch-and-release long before it became as popular as it is now. He lobbied successfully for the first no-kill river section ever designated in Colorado—a stretch of the Roaring Fork upstream from the upper Woody Creek bridge. Today, that section is a public park set aside primarily for fly-fishermen, and shortly after his death, friends and family made plans to place a plaque there to honor Chuck.

Chuck succumbed to cancer at his home near the river in 1996 after successfully fighting off an earlier attack of prostate cancer. With typical Fothergill thoughtfulness and practicality, he used his experience with the prostate problem to film a television spot urging men to have prostate checkups.

In 1970, when I assumed the job of outdoor editor of the *Denver Post*, it was on one condition that I didn't particularly like. For at least a while, I would have to double as the paper's ski editor. The "while" turned out to be almost three years, but I visited some interesting places and met some fascinating people in that time. One of those people was Chuck Fothergill. He lived and worked in Aspen in those days. One cloudy but relatively mild day in early March, I found myself driving back along Colorado 82 near Basalt, returning from coverage of an Aspen ski race. At that time, fly-fishing to me was a summer and autumn sport. I didn't get really serious about it until after spring runoff, and I usually put away the rods about the time the waterfowl hunting seasons opened.

To my astonishment, as I rounded a bend where the river cut close to the highway embankment, I spotted three wader-clad fly-fishermen standing strung out in a long run, the far side of which featured an undercut bank and a stand of cottonwood trees. The man in the middle was fighting a fish. I stopped the car at the first pullout, shaking my head in amazement at this winter vision of madmen fishing with fly rods—and actually hooking something. I had to find out what they were doing.

The man with the bent rod was Chuck Fothergill, and the fish he was bringing to net for release was a seventeen-inch brown. "How's it going?" I called out. Chuck waded over, and we introduced ourselves. "It's going rather well," he said. "That's about the fifteenth trout we've hooked in this run." The brown had taken a No. 14 gold-ribbed Hare's Ear, one of Fothergill's favorite patterns. He paused in his fishing to give a brief explanation of how he was fishing it.

That was my first introduction to the wonders of winter nymphing on the Roaring Fork. A few weeks later, I joined Chuck for a day of fishing on the Woody Creek water, and it was to be the first of many enjoyable and educational days spent with this red-haired, freckle-faced man over the next two decades. We sort of lost touch in the few years preceding his death, and I regret that. But I was blessed with getting more than one lesson in floating-line nymphing from Chuck Fothergill. He had first used this technique on the South Platte River when he lived in the Denver area, and he perfected it to a fine art on the Roaring Fork.

I remember one of those early days with Chuck on the Fork, when he outfished me by a wide margin. We retired to a Basalt bar for beers, where I asked simply, "What was I doing wrong?" What followed was a gracious, priceless, point-by-point short course on the tackle, mechanics, and strategy of "the Colorado method." Nothing pertinent was left out, and his tips filled several pages of my steno notepad. They were passed on in increments to the readers of the *Denver Post*. I know those readers were grateful. I certainly was.

The Roaring Fork, of course, is more than just a nymph-fishing river, and there is more to fly-fishing than dead-drifting a nymph pattern near bottom with a floating line. As this technique gained fame and acceptance among millions of anglers, strike indicators slipped onto the leader more or less became part of the tackle scheme. But in the times I fished with Fothergill, I never saw him use an indicator. The end of his fly line and the leader butt itself were his indicators.

The dead-drift technique has become so pervasive and is so effective much of the time that it has come to be derided in some fly-fishing circles. "Dredging bottom" is a common put-down, but there is no arguing that it has made it possible for countless anglers to take countless fish anywhere trout exist in moving water, often under conditions that aren't conducive to other methods.

The Roaring Fork is an underrated and challenging stream, partly because of its many spread-out, fast-water sections. But those who learn to read it, and who ferret out the private landowners who are willing to give fishing permission, can expect to do well. One characteristic of the river is that it is very difficult water in which to sight-fish to specific trout, unless they are feeding at the surface. This is largely because of the checkerboard design of the bottom rocks, which consist of basalt, quartzite, and limestone. It is a perfectly camouflaged, mosaic backdrop for fish, and of all the trout or whitefish that I have caught from the Roaring Fork, I cannot remember seeing a single one of them first unless they were breaking the surface. The upshot is that being able to read the water is even more critical than it is on many other rivers.

Summer and fall anglers on the Roaring Fork take very nice trout, and lots of them, on dry flies, shallow wet flies, and streamers when shirtsleeve weather settles over the valley and the river is at medium flow. There is a blizzardlike caddisfly hatch in early May and a Green Drake hatch in the summer. Later, in the fall, low flows spell very spooky trout and the fishing becomes tougher. Trout sometimes can be taken with remarkable success on tiny midge-type dry flies, even in the dead of winter.

But in my mind, "the Colorado method" of nymphing was made for the tricky currents of the Roaring Fork, particularly in winter, and vice versa. That it has become a fundamental approach on rivers throughout the West is a tribute to the Roaring Fork and to the man who sang the praises of the river and the method.

THE adaptable angler

part THREE

CHAPTER 9

MYSIS MANIA

THERE ARE ONLY TWO COMPELLING CONSIDERATIONS THAT COULD induce a fly-fisherman to fish in a toilet bowl or underneath an interstate highway bridge. One is trout. The second is bigger trout. Trout can be found in a lot of places, and most of them are beautiful. That's one of the bonuses of fishing for trout. But probably everyone has fished for trout in less-than-pristine settings, simply because the fish were there.

One of the factors that produces big trout is an abundance of food. And one food type that really does the job is a kind of steroidal tidbit known imprecisely by most anglers as "mysis shrimp." The cholesterol content on these critters has to be higher, relatively speaking, than a four-topping pizza. The mysis—a shrimplike crustacean found in both fresh and salt water—can cause salmonids to become freakishly big in relatively short spans of time.

Which is what led Pat Dorsey, Scott Ratcliff, and I to bundle ourselves and our gear into my Ford Bronco on a crisp, clear March day in Colorado and point the vehicle west out Interstate 70 from Denver toward the mountain town of Silverthorne and the Blue River. The Blue drains a high-mountain valley, one that is plastered in sometimes obscene randomness with condos and ski lodges, just west of the Continental Divide. To me, making this day trip was mostly a lark, although I knew well enough the potential of mysis, escaping through dams from the deep water of reservoirs, to foster outlandish, football-shaped trout (mostly rainbows) in certain tailwaters.

Which is where the "toilet bowl" comes in. "Toilet bowl" is the cynical name that was given by fly-fishermen to the first afterbay-type plunge hole just below the outlet of Ruedi Dam on the Frying Pan River. There, overstuffed rainbows as big as twenty pounds hang in tantalizing suspension in currents that carry to them the helpless, whitish-translucent mysis in pig-out numbers. The mysis factor holds sway for as much as a mile below the dam. It's catch-and-release on rainbows, and some of these hogs have been caught and turned loose so many times that Frying Pan regulars have anointed them with nicknames and can identify them through Polaroids from thirty feet away. "There's Herman; there's Old Scar Face"— that sort of thing.

A similar freak show plays to packed-house audiences of wader-clad fans in less than a half-mile of public catch-and-release water on the Taylor River immediately below Taylor Park Dam, northeast of Gunnison. The drill is simple enough: Take a number, then take your shot, usually with a mysis imitation or a tiny midge larva pattern on no larger than a 5X tippet—and get a good grip on your nerves. The trout you are casting to and that you can see clearly usually weighs at least five pounds. Ten-pounders raise few eyebrows on the Frying Pan and Taylor tailwaters.

Word that mysis mania had arrived on the Blue River, however, was a new twist on the freak factor. We knew that mysis had been dumped, once upon a time, in Dillon Reservoir on the Blue in a desperate effort to feed the reservoir's undernourished browns. The bathtublike water-level fluctuations of the reservoir had played havoc over the years with the once-rich insect and crustacean life of the weedy, shallow bays. All the mysis did, however, was scarf up what was left of the plankton, further sterilizing the lake. Rumors that they were finally getting washed out to create a Blue (River) Heaven for lunker hunters were new to us. And, of course, such rumors must be checked out.

Which is where the interstate bridge comes in. I figured that my most useful piece of gear on this little foray into cabin-fever whimsy would be a lawn chair. It would provide a nice perch from which to kibitz while my partners probed diligently for nonexistent monsters. Somehow, I couldn't envision twenty- to thirty-inch rainbows or browns in the Blue, which, until relatively recent stockings of wild, fingerling, Colorado River–strain rainbows, had been little more than a fairly good brown-trout stream and a dumping ground for the state wildlife division's beloved "catchable-size" stocker rainbows. But attitudes about the Blue had begun to change. Even the town fathers in Silverthorne were beginning to envision their piece of the river as a stream with wild-trout and big-trout promise. They had rebuffed a state move to liberalize the creel limits and method regulations (bait isn't legal). They insisted on, and got, a no-kill rule on the two miles through the city limits. After the whirling-disease crisis began to devastate wild rainbow trout around the state in the early 1990s, these Silverthorne visionaries even rejected a state plan to stock about 100,000 hatchery rainbows—fish exposed to the parasite—in Dillon Reservoir. Taken in the context of Colorado towns that thrive on tourism, this is roughly like tellers refusing to accept deposits at bank windows.

Still, when we pulled off the main drag, turned left at the Seven Eleven (or was it the Burger King?) and angled over to come to a stop in a gravelly parking area underneath the steel girders of the interstate bridge, I couldn't help but laugh. Vehicles whizzed by on nearby streets, kids riding skateboards careened down a streamside bike path, and factory-store shoppers were parking their cars in a paved lot on the other side of the river. They had their sights trained on fur coats; we were shopping for something just as gaudy and a lot harder to find. As we emerged from the car and gathered tackle, the girderwork on the bridge over our heads hummed with the rumbling passage of huge semitrailer trucks.

Ah, I thought, the exhilarating sights and sounds of a wild trout stream.

Tongue firmly positioned in cheek, I propped up my trusty lawn chair, plopped down in it, and began to go through the motions of assembling tackle and donning insulated waders. It was about noon and the air temperature had struggled bravely into the forties—a veritable heat wave in this ice-box valley. Hip-deep snowbanks glistened brilliantly under an intense, almost blinding sun. Perfect conditions for fooling large trout, right? Hardly, even if you labored under the shaky assumption that the rumors were true and the big trout actually existed.

I still hadn't bothered to put on the waders when Dorsey and Ratcliff, graphite rods clutched resolutely in mitten-clad hands, slogged through the snow toward a shadowy run under the steel girders.

"You're gonna fish, aren't you?" Pat said.

"Write if you find work," I said noncommitally. I considered reaching into the cooler for a beer and rejected the notion. I might be violating some city ordinance.

As it turned out, Pat found work right away. If you can call casting to outrageously sized, prespawning-mode rainbows in clear currents, work.

"Bob, you won't believe this," he called as he waded into position. "There must be a dozen trout in this run, and the smallest one I see is about sixteen inches long."

"How big is the biggest one?" I called back, playing along but reaching for the waders just in case.

"You won't believe it," he said, repetitiously.

Actually, I started believing it after I saw Pat's three-weight rod, rigged with floating line, a long, 6X-tippet leader, strike indicator, and a black midge larva pattern, dip suddenly and begin doing a convulsive dance in doubled-over cadence. The rod flashed in the sunlight, as did the gaudily colored, roughly three-pound rainbow he eventually slid into his landing net. Slightly upstream, Scott was wide-eyed as he cast his offering to another group of broad-shouldered rainbows.

What ensued was a madcap winter interlude of sight fishing to rainbows running from two to at least eight pounds, with frequent hookups, intermittent broken tippets, and enough actual landings of these football-shaped fish to cause us to conclude that we had, indeed, found our Blue Heaven. I say eight pounds, because that was the approximate weight of the largest rainbow we landed and released. It was a red-flanked, gorgeously hued male fish to which Pat had cast for a good ten minutes before the trout, for some reason, moodily shifted position and came upstream toward me. Mostly by chance, the cast I made with a two-fly rig of a small San Juan Worm about twenty inches above a Black Midge (No. 22) on a 6X dropper fell almost precisely where it had to in order to pass directly in front of the snout of the now-feeding rainbow. I saw the flash of his side as he took one of the flies, and I saw the red strike indicator go under.

"I got the big one," I whooped after setting the hook. The word "got" was presumptuously premature, but it sounded good.

"Holy shit," was what Pat said.

Holy shit, for sure. What I had to figure out, now that I had hooked this holy-shit fish, was what to do with it. The rainbow was steaming downstream toward the lip of a rock check dam, one of the stream-improvement structures that the wildlife division and various volunteers had recently created. The locals in town called them "trout condos."

This fish looked like it was ready to swim right over the condo, and there was not much I could do about it on a 6X tippet made weaker by its knotted hinge at the upper, bigger fly. The rainbow had taken the point fly—the midge imitation. (Eventually, we concluded that the mysis patterns, paradoxically enough, didn't work as well as the midge-type patterns. Apparently, the crustaceans weren't in one of their flush-out modes.) In a burst of brilliant (and blind-pig lucky) improvisation, I bowed the rod to the running trout and gave it slack line. There was no way I could force it back from the check dam and my aging, arthritic knees wouldn't allow a mad dash over ice-slick streambed rocks anymore.

The ploy worked. The rainbow stopped above the rock ledge, turned as if he thought he was free, and came back upstream toward me. After that, it was a matter of tiring the trout, which was easy enough to do because these fish were relatively sluggish in the forty-degree water.

All of us had some fun catching and releasing fish normally found either in our dreams or in faraway waters, including a seven-pound male rainbow landed by Dorsey. That fish was almost an exact replica of the big one I had been fortunate enough to land. Somewhere in the mix were a couple of browns in the two- to three-pound class.

When we returned happily to the vehicle, the forgotten lawn chair had a coating of frost on it—maybe from the exhaust of the trucks and cars passing by overhead. "Can you believe this?" Dorsey said in wonderment, looking back at the run full of lunkers.

"Was there ever a doubt?" I said, straight-faced.

You can look at this head-hunting for mysis-stuffed monsters in one of two main ways. You can consider it a circus sideshow in the otherwise real world of Colorado stream fishing, to be indulged in when you don't mind the surroundings of other frenziedly focused head-hunters all around you, or, in the case of the Blue, the noise and clutter of a Western Slope minicity in ski-resort country. In this context, you can decide that it's not for you and that it resembles the essence of fly-fishing for trout no more closely than a romance novel resembles a Shakespeare play.

You even can lament what has happened on the Frying Pan, which once upon a time was a nice, little, relatively unsung stream in the cedar- and conifer-covered red-rock ridges not far from Aspen, a fifteen-mile stretch of water that was always generous with insect hatches and trout that averaged thirteen to seventeen inches in length. It has become increasingly hard to find a stretch of privately owned water on the Frying Pan that isn't either under lease or tightly posted to everyone. It has become virtually impossible to fish out of sight of another angler on public sections of the Pan, particularly in the mysis tailwater section.

Taking the other view, you can shrug philosophically and get in line, knowing that there are few other places in the West where steelhead-size trout feed on crustaceans or other drifting morsels, some of which are no larger than a grain of rice. And you know that you'll have a very good chance to hook a few of them, even if some of these battle-hardened veterans seem to roll over and submit halfway into the fight, as if saying to themselves, "Not this shit again." The trout you land may have hook scars all over its jaws.

Maybe the sensible way to approach this is with a balanced view. It's different, it's fun, it's exciting, but for most folks, it isn't something that is going to take the place of—as it has for some trophy-obsessed egos—an out-of-the-way canyon stream, for instance, that offers solitude and relatively naive trout that are much smaller but respond to much larger offerings. So you do the mysis routine once in a while, just to keep your hand in and experience the thrill of fishing to fantastically large trout.

The largest, officially recorded mysis-fed monster to be hooked and landed in a Colorado tailwater to date was a twenty-two-and-one-half-pound rainbow, taken and released on the Taylor River by Brian Byerly of Lakewood, Colorado. The angler measured and photographed the trout and submitted it to the Master Angler Awards Program of the Colorado Division of Wildlife. The program recognizes the biggest fish (measured in length) caught and released in state waters. The weight of Byerly's fish was estimated by means of a standard mathematical formula incorporating length and girth measurements.

There are vague stories of bigger rainbows taken and released on both the Taylor and the Frying Pan. Most of these are exaggerated estimates, no doubt, but one fly shop on the Frying Pan has a mounted, twenty-five-pound rainbow that was found dead in the Ruedi tailwater section. All of this, on the surface, might lead to the question of why the state biologists don't dump mysis into every cold-water reservoir around or, for that matter, scatter them like fertilizer into the length and breadth of every major trout stream. Then we'd have gutbusters all over the place.

Well, for one thing, these shrimplike creatures—originally imported to Colorado from Minnesota—haven't quite worked out the way they were supposed to in reservoirs. In some of the reservoirs where they were introduced (as a hoped-for forage for species such as rainbow trout, brown trout, lake trout, and kokanee salmon), they had a backfire effect. They weren't available much of the time to the fish they were supposed to feed, because the mysis migrate vertically at extremely varying depths. Much of the time, they're either below the fish or suspended away from them. Second, mysis live on plankton, and the plankton are the linchpins of the fragile food chain. What used to be prolific kokanee salmon populations at reservoirs like Dillon and Granby quickly became remnant, stunted populations when their plankton supply was preempted by mysis. Finally, freshwater mysis—the only freshwater representative of a huge order of crustaceans that primarily live in oceans or bays—die when they enter flowing water. Therefore, the sole benefit in a river is in the mile or two below a dam, when they haplessly get washed out.

As mentioned earlier, many of these mysis-fat lunkers are taken not on mysis imitations—although a few effective ones have been conceived—but on tiny midge larva or emerger patterns, or equally tiny mayfly nymph patterns. As biologists explain it, the mysis, in their migrations, may at times be in the vicinity of the deep outlet structures of dams but at other times may not be in any danger of getting flushed into the river. Mysis patterns varying in size from No. 12 to No. 18, with No. 16 a good average, can work well during flush-out periods, although some fishermen believe that success with a mysis pattern is compromised by the fact that the artificial is competing with so many naturals.

Mysis patterns are usually crafted out of some sort of synthetic—sometimes out of the transparent material that makes up Baggie or Glad Wrap–type products. The effect is a glistening translucency that gives what would seem to be a realistic image, although another theory holds that when mysis die—as they do shortly after being ejected into a tailwater—they turn a more opaque white.

Most mysis-tailwater fly-fishing is accomplished with dead-drift tactics that incorporate floating fly line, long leaders, strike indicators, and a bit of weight above the fly or flies but not enough to sink the indicator. One accomplished angler and flytier I know, however, believes that most mysis caught up in a river current float without swimming or moving, staying near the surface. Accordingly, he fishes mysis patterns without any weight.

Perhaps the more dependable approach is midging, if for no other reason than midges constitute the more predictable, day-in, day-out trout fare on a stream in winter or early spring, which are the best times to pursue mysis monsters. The water is lower and more easily fished, the trout are more concentrated and easily spotted, and there are fewer competing anglers around.

Midge larva or pupa patterns, as well as mayfly nymph imitations, should be tiny—no larger than hook size 18 and sometimes as small as 24 or 26. Seasoned tailwater experts in Colorado favor these patterns: the Black Midge (or, as Pat Dorsey calls his version, the Black Beauty, ribbed with fine copper wire), the Red Disco Midge, WD-40, South Platte Brassie, Biot Midge, Buckskin, RS-2, the San Juan Emerger, and the Pheasant Tail. Some fishermen use a standard two-fly rig incorporating either a couple of these choices or one of them below a tan or pink-colored San Juan Worm. Occasionally, a big trout is duped by the worm pattern, but most anglers believe it serves as an attractor that leads the selective fish to the smaller pattern.

There is general agreement that in clear, heavily pressured water, these big trout have seen so many fishermen and so many lines and leaders that a downstream, dead-drift presentation, with line-feeding and line-mending tactics, has the best chance to fool them. That way, they see the fly first, not the leader or line.

To mysis-fed waters, the angler should bring an open mind, high hopes, a low silhouette, and, if he likes, some form of tranquilizer—perhaps the liquid variety that comes in a bottle. He'll need it to calm himself—or celebrate later. Perhaps both.

CHAPTER 10

THE NEW ICE AGE

WHEN MARK ARMSTRONG FINISHED PUTTING UP THE TENTLIKE ice-fishing shelter, he left me to thaw out in its relatively toasty confines while he shuffled over the ice, seemingly without purpose, toward a rocky point closer to the shoreline of Elevenmile Reservoir. The early morning sky was dazzlingly blue. There was no wind. It was all very pretty, but the air temperature was five degrees below zero.

I misinterpreted Armstrong's bequeathment of the small shelter as entirely a noble gesture. I assumed he was worried about the wimpy outdoor writer coming down with a case of cold feet (not to mention ears, fingers, nose, and other assorted frozen body parts, some of them very personal and prone to shrinkage).

The shelter was out in about forty feet of water, a good fifty yards from shore. It was a spot where we expected, sometime during the morning, to find rainbow trout and kokanee salmon suspended at fifteen to twenty feet, which is the depth Armstrong calculated for the plankton level. As it turned out later, his calculation was correct. We were to catch several fish of both species under precisely that scenario.

But for now, Armstrong, a maker of ice rods, reels, and jigs who is generally recognized as the modern-day guru of Colorado ice fishing (the word is overworked, but it does fit), knew something I didn't. Although it was late February and still very much winter in the vast, stark mountain basin known as South Park, big rainbow trout were already moving toward the shallower water of small, rock- and gravel-bottomed bays in search of spawning territory. Early in the spawning season, they prowl these areas at first light but re-treat to deeper haunts when the sun is high.

Just about the time I was summoning sympathy for my ex-posed-to-the-elements partner and thinking to wax expansive and invite him inside with me, I heard him yell. I stiffly lurched outside onto the snow-covered, twenty-six-inch-thick ice with camera in hand—the abominable ice man with a Nikon. Armstrong was hunched over a hole, his light, whippy glass ice rod bent double and violently bouncing toward the water in the hole like a divining rod.

"This," Mark said, his panting breath sending a cloud of va-por into the air, "is a hell of a trout."

So it was. When he finally threw frostbite caution to the wind and thrust his hand down into the water of the hole, he hoisted out a ten-pound male rainbow that was the most gor-geously colored lake rainbow I had ever seen. A 1/32-ounce, chartreuse, chenille-body-and-marabou-tail jig was lodged solidly in the corner of its prominent jaw. The give-and-take fight on four-pound-test line had lasted at least ten minutes.

The ten minutes had been long enough to freeze the shut-ter of my camera. I punched frantically at the shutter button and was rewarded with a low, grinding noise. Sometimes our gadgetry is as much at the mercy of the elements as we are—which is sort of reassuring, in a way.

"Does this," Mark asked, holding up the gleaming, olive-and-maroon-flanked, darkly spotted trout, "make the discom-fort worthwhile, or what? And people wonder why anybody ice fishes." Yes, they do. As a matter of fact, I was one of those people at one time. Of all God's creations, the enigmatic, masochistic, obsessed individuals known as ice fishermen may be the strangest. They are accused, perhaps justifiably, of being a couple of eggs short of an intellectual omelet. These eccentrics start quivering with anticipation when the late-fall, overnight temperatures dip below fifteen degrees. A pro-longed, zero to subzero spell, from their perspective, is cause for jubilant celebration.

Ice fishermen—God love 'em. Their wives and children and non-ice-fishing friends do, too, but only from safe distances when the lake surfaces freeze. They are not necessarily welcomed with open arms when they stagger home with a sackful of trout or still-flopping perch and a suspicious hint of schnapps on their breath. Tolerantly, ice fishermen look upon these assorted noncombatants as summer soldiers and sunshine patriots. They accept it when these jelly-backboned bystanders disdain to partake in the smelly, slippery business of filleting orange-meat trout or white-meat perch but somehow magically appear at the dinner table when the finished product is presented. These non-ice-fishermen gladly help you dispose of a platter of fried fillets, but they wouldn't walk out onto a frozen lake to watch Ann-Margret ice fish in a bikini. (Hell, I'd crawl out there if I had to.) Or if they do walk out there, it's just to get a closer look at these perverted characters. To them, ice fishing is a spectator sport, and it's okay to leave at halftime.

Suffice it to say that the lure and lore of ice fishing is lost on some folks, including a lot of them who fish avidly at warmer times of the year. There is this persistent perception, even among other fishermen, that ice fishing is just some let's-get-out-of-the-house ritual during which everybody stands or sits around waiting for a flag to pop up or somebody to pass the brandy flask. The idea that it can involve specialized light tackle and tactics and actually result in the catching of a lot of fish is not universally embraced.

But in the colder climes—particularly in the western states, where light-tackle ice fishing is a relatively new phenomenon—the hard-water clan grows by leaps and bounds, and tip-ups aren't the equipment of choice. (In fact, a tip-up spread may be illegal—typically, in western states, having more than two lines in the water is against regulations.) This surge is propelled by the revelation that you actually *can* catch fish this way if you take the same sort of thoughtful, scientific approach to it that you do when standing in your favorite trout stream and contriving to match the hatch.

Thoughtful? Scientific? Are these words that can actually be connected in the same sentence with ice fishing? Yes, they can, although many people still have serious misgivings about it.

I am reminded of the day when Don Murphy and I sat on our upended five-gallon paint buckets (an antitechnology fashion statement) and cranked fish after fish onto the ice of Denver's Cherry Creek Reservoir—plump yellow perch and hand-sized crappies tightly schooled at slightly varying depths over a bottom hump. They responded to 1/64-ounce or smaller marabou-tail jigs dangled two to eight feet off bottom with short ice rods and three-pound-test monofilament line. An accidental tourist happened by—one of those people who treat cabin fever by walking out onto the ice to see what these nuts are up to with their buckets, sleds, and pygmy rods. This guy shuffled over to Murphy, stared down at the pile of fish next to the eight-inch-diameter hole, and said, "Did you catch all those fish *here?*" To which Murphy, with his dry Irish wit, replied, "No, we brought them with us."

The poet, novelist, and angler Jim Harrison once dismissed ice fishing as "the moronic sport." Maybe so. It's hard to explain the allure of this odd outdoor enterprise. You have to get into all sorts of esoteric stuff about pristine winter landscapes and the quiet of a snow-covered ice cap—but I think at the core of it, there's an analogy to golf. In golf, the little white ball with dimples in it is the great equalizer. Starting out in the game, superbly conditioned young athletes can't score any lower than a fifty-year-old accountant with a potbelly and arthritic knees. The great equalizer in ice fishing is the ice. Nobody has the advantage because he owns a boat or a float tube or a $600 rod or a garage full of high-tech equipment, or even because he possesses an arcane ability to "read the water." In ice fishing, there is nothing on the surface to read, unless it is a cluster of frozen-over holes left the day before by somebody who got into a concentration of fish. ("Look at those cigarette butts—somebody must have spent some time here.")

So everybody sets out on equal footing, literally. This isn't to say that being equipped the right way, knowing the depths and configurations of the lake bottom and understanding the tendencies of ice-bound fish don't count for something. It all counts for a lot to the Renaissance ice angler. Somebody who knows his stuff can walk out onto the ice with his plastic bucket, a $50 auger, a $20 glass rod that's shorter than his leg, a $30 reel, a $3.50 lake-bottom topo map, 30 yards of light mono line, a small box of jigs, maybe a little container of mealworms or maggots with which to tip the jigs, and a $5 ice skimmer, and catch more fish in a winter season than a summertime angler with $5,000 worth of tackle and a $30,000 boat.

The one exception to this rule of antitechnology in ice fishing is the matter of portable sonar units. In winter under the ice, fish generally aren't scattered like they are in spring and summer. They tend to bunch up or suspend at favored depths and in preferred places, depending on water oxygen content, bottom contours, water temperature, and availability of forage. Owning a portable "fish finder" can speed up the process of prospecting for fish under the ice and cut down considerably on the muscle power required to drill a number of holes. Sometimes these devices save you the frustration of fishing ten feet below or ten feet above a concentration of fish suspended at a certain depth. Some ice fishermen even use the more sensitive of these liquid-crystal-type units to detect when a fish is about to take the lure or a bait. It is possible to see the blip of the fish homing in like a missile to the blip of the bait or lure—a sort of computer-age vision of what is taking place under the ice.

I grant that this is a form of visual stimulation and a technological edge, but I don't do it. If I use a sonar, it's to find fish, not to detect strikes. To me, fishing isn't a video game. Or if it is, my video is a very inexpensive, very low-tech device known popularly as a "wire indicator" or "spring bobber." This ingenious little accessory can be purchased in hobby or tackle shops for anywhere from twenty-five cents to a buck-fifty, depending on whether it's in finished-product form or not. What it consists of is about a six-inch-long piece of piano wire, or modeling wire, soldered into a loop at the end. What it becomes is a highly sensitive extension rod tip attached to the end of the regular rod. The line is strung through the rod guides and tip-top guide and then out through the loop of the wire extension. The slightest hit, nudge, kiss, tap, or inhalation of the lure or bait by a fish results in a corresponding flex, jerk, or dip in the wire-indicator rod tip. Strikes that wouldn't register in a regular rod tip are graphically telegraphed into the wire. Casual ice anglers who haven't yet discovered "the wire" get lots of strikes, too. They just don't know it.

The wire indicator has revolutionized ice angling and helped take it from the heavy-duty business of running several tip-ups into the realm of light tackle sport. In a way, the wire holds the same charm, if that's the right word, as a tip-up. The flag goes up or the wire goes down and that means fish. Most guys paint their wire tips a fluorescent orange or red, the better to detect the sometimes minute movements of the wire that telegraph the presence of a striking fish down in the depths.

Staring at the wire evolves into a mesmerizing duty—a kind of zenlike trance. The sheer concentration required in serious ice fishing is a total escape from the outside world. I have seen this intense concentration mirrored in the faces of ice anglers in places as diverse as perch-populated gravel pits and major reservoirs holding trophy-class lake trout. I know the feeling. I find myself suddenly looking up from the little wire loop at the end of the rod and realize that it takes a second to refocus my eyes on anything farther than six feet away.

My ice-fishing buddy, Murphy, refers to this as "the thousand-yard stare." He makes it sound like combat. I suppose in a remote sense, when the elements are less than comforting, it is. The fight, at times, is with the elements. Even Leonard Wright, author of books and magazine pieces on the nuances of dry-fly fishing for trout, alluded to it in a story he once did on ice fishing for the *New York Times*.

He described how he felt after his first ice-fishing expedition: "As I approached my car I was surprised to realize that my chin was out and that, despite my numb feet, I was strutting a bit . . . the way fighter pilots probably do when they've just returned from their private perilous place and start walking back to the everyday world of the ready room."

Any attempt to explain the fascination of an aspect of out-door sport is subjective, difficult, and, by definition, probably futile. I don't believe that the macho aspect of ice fishing is the compelling ingredient in the stew. Rather, for me, it is the visual imagery. If the height of pleasure in outdoor pursuits is directly proportional to the simplicity and purity of the experience, then ice fishing definitely qualifies. You sit there, when there is snow on the ice, in a world of cold, pure whiteness, listening to the wind or the cry of migrating geese or the screeching of scavenging gulls, and the core of your very existence becomes the bright red tip of the wire strike indicator on the end of the rod. You are taken back to the times you spent as a child, watching the cork bobber with the worm or the grasshopper dangling underneath it in the mysterious depths of the pond, waiting with expectancy and unwavering faith, fully confident that the bobber would soon twitch, jiggle, and then dive beneath the surface.

On the ice, that bright bead at the end of the wire becomes your bobber, your world, your epicenter, your reason for being alive. And when it moves, you move, and underneath the ice the fish moves so that you feel it all the way through the rod into your soul. Some unspoken but very profound promise has been fulfilled. You have bridged the real and yet symbolic barrier embodied in the ice cap, the frozen separation—a wall of aloofness almost like the lid of a coffin—between life above the ice and life below it. The pervasive death embodied by winter has been repelled or at least delayed. The inexorable drilling of the auger, or the pounding penetration of the ice spud, are like the wooden stake into the vampire's heart. There is life down there, and you have made a connection with it.

In his description of the ice-fishing fanatics he observed, Len Wright also asked this rhetorical question: "Were they the counterparts of the solitary and fishless fishermen on the Seine in Paris who are reputed to be getting away from their wives? Was there exhilaration in sheer survival?"

No, Len, not entirely. There is exhilaration not just in survival, but in defying the implied paralysis of winter, in mastery of a form of fishing that is, or can be, every bit as productive as being there in warmer times, when bass blast into a school of shad or trout gorge on a mayfly hatch.

When the ice men cometh, it's not just survival of the fittest. It's a triumph of the adaptable.

CHAPTER 11
BEING THERE

CHARLIE MEYERS IS LOUNGING IN THE FRONT SEAT OF THE Bronco, happily and unhurriedly liberating the contents of a bottle of very good chardonnay. The wine had been a windfall, left in the kitchen of our day-rented Steamboat Springs condo as a complimentary gesture by the condo manager. We don't know it at the moment, but we are about to be the beneficiaries of another windfall. I decline his offer of more of the good grape, wolf down the last of my ham sandwich, and walk around to the back of the vehicle to rig up a rod and tug on some waders.

We are parked in a spot overlooking one of the west-side bays of Stagecoach Reservoir, a relatively new impoundment as Colorado reservoirs go. The dam on the Yampa River about fifteen miles southeast of Steamboat Springs created a modest-sized lake surrounded by sagebrush ridges. Meyers, with the serenity that comes from years of experience on high-elevation trout lakes and sophisticated enough to have a deep appreciation for the finer products of California vineyards, is not terribly intent on rushing directly down to the water. We both know that on blue-sky summer days, as this one is, serious action on shoreline-prowling trout often doesn't begin until late in the day. Or, it comes early in the day, and we have already missed that opportunity.

But I am beginning to see rises out on the smooth surface of the shallow, weed-bottomed, elliptical-shaped bay, and they appear to be increasing in number. Leaving Charlie to his blissful and extended lunch break, I trudge down through the sagebrush and wade in. I have tied a dry fly to my 5X leader tippet.

Fifteen minutes and two fly changes later, I am still strike-less. But rainbow trout are slashing at the surface all over the bay, the most frenetic of the activity coming during calm interludes between stirrings of a breeze. I am totally puzzled about what is going on until I pause to stare at the surface of the shallows to see if I can identify a particular hatch that might be coming off. I see no insects other than the scattered remains of a minor midge hatch, and that doesn't seem to jibe with the aggressiveness of the trout.

I am looking so hard for some evidence of an insect hatch that it takes me a minute to get a grasp of the bigger picture: Floating around me in the disarray that comes with fish-feeding carnage are the dead or dying remains of a school of fathead minnows. Then I notice that the survivors—small minnows about an inch to an inch and a half long—are darting in panic in less than a foot of water, right up against the bank. That is their only refuge from rainbow trout ranging in size from twelve to seventeen inches—trout that are for all the world looking and acting like a horde of small stripers blasting into a school of shad.

Simultaneously, I remember the guy in the Steamboat Springs fly shop who had insisted that morning that we take along a few samples of a gaudy, white-and-silver streamer fly pattern the shop calls a "Liberace." It is clear now why he had given this advice. The small streamer—actually, a flashy version of a Woolly Bugger—is a reasonable facsimile of the hapless baitfish trapped in this cove. I tie on a Liberace, execute a forty-foot cast across the center of the cove, and make exactly two strips of the floating fly line before a fourteen-inch rainbow jolts the streamer to a rude halt.

A now rigged and ready Meyers is at my side a few minutes later, grinning beatifically either from the mellowing effects of the wine or the realization that his partner is regularly hooking trout. He has shown up just about the time I am landing and releasing my third rainbow. "What the hell is happening? Are these trout suicidal?" he inquires.

"Believe it or not, these trout are gorging on minnows. Tie on one of your Liberaces."

"One of my what?"

The upshot is that we spend three delightful hours in that grassy bay, nailing rainbow after rainbow on Liberaces and other light-colored streamer concoctions, until a violent late-afternoon lightning storm sends us retreating back to the Bronco.

The phenomenon of minnow-chasing rainbow trout is so unusual to us that it is most of what we talk about for the first hour or so on the drive back to Denver. Years of fishing mountain lakes has taught us that rainbows seldom make use of minnow populations; that propensity usually is attributed to brown or cutthroat trout. In fact, there are reservoirs in Colorado where rainbows grow very slowly because they somehow fail, or refuse, to utilize abundant minnow populations that stick close to the bank in shallow water. But when it comes to reservoir trout behavior, just about anything is possible at any given time. The message brings to mind a Peter Sellers movie that has become a sort of cult icon among film fanciers. The movie was a comedy about a retarded gardener who, through an unlikely sequence of circumstances that places him in exactly the right spots at the right times, rises to the level of personal advisor to the President of the United States. The title of the movie was *Being There*.

It would make a good title, too, for a book about fishing mountain reservoirs in reference to timing. Sometimes, success is less a matter of going through a checklist of empirical angling approaches than it is of simply being on the water at the right time of day or week or month—being fortunate or shrewd enough to be present when some positive triggering mechanism comes into play, and being able to interpret it and adjust to it.

The minnow-massacre phenomenon is rare, and I have never since that day seen rainbows gathered in loosely organized schools, attacking minnows in the shallows like a pack of hungry sharks. (I did see something similar to it once on Nevada's Wildhorse Reservoir, but the feeding was more scattered.) Much more predictably, trout key into insect hatches such as midges, mayflies, or damselflies, or crustaceans such as shrimp or sowbugs. They may grab the odd minnow or small trout if it strays into their territory, but "herding" of bait fish isn't on their list of preferred tactics.

Once, fishing a similar weedy bay at Steamboat Lake, twenty-five miles north of Steamboat Springs, three of us were hooking an occasional rainbow, but were beginning to get the feeling that our ratio of hookups to feeding trout was woefully in arrears. It was a sunny, warm day in June. Wading back to shore to retrieve a beer from a cooler, I was surprised to see a rainbow trout of about fifteen inches lying motionless in less than six inches of water, tight up against the overhanging grass of the bank. My first thought was that this fish was sick or perhaps had been caught and released earlier by one of us and hadn't fully recovered. But then the rainbow darted about two feet to one side and obviously captured some form of prey. It went back to its station but spooked when it saw my silhouette.

It wasn't until I had observed two more trout behaving in exactly the same manner that it finally came to me—damselflies. Damsels hatch in early summer, swimming in erratic, darting movements into shallow water and then up to the shore or partly submerged sticks, logs, and weeds, where they crawl out in the manner of stoneflies. It was obvious that the migration was in progress and that the optimum ambush point for enterprising trout was in the shallowest water.

After switching to olive damsel nymphs, we began to hook trout with outrageous repetition by casting into the shallows parallel to the shoreline. This action continued well into the early evening hours, and when we finally trudged up the hill to the waiting vehicle, the tally of trout hooked and released by three fly-fishermen was probably around the six-dozen mark. An overindulgence bordering on the obscene, perhaps, but a classic case of "being there."

Being there and figuring it out is easy when the damsels hatch, because the hatch can occur over a period of two weeks or more. It is less a test of pattern selection than it is of fishing the right water—weedy or grassy shallows—and making the right retrieve. The basic routine is short, erratic strips followed by pauses to let the fly sink a moment. I have fished with remarkably elaborate imitations of damselfly nymphs, complete with eyeballs and elbows, and they work pretty well at times. But precise imitation is not necessary and basically a waste of tying time or fly-purchase money. One of the more effective damsel nymph imitations, in my experience, is a very rough generalization of the insect. In Colorado, it's referred to as a Gray Ugly, but it travels under various other aliases in other states. It has a body of peacock herl, with fore-and-aft grizzly hackle. It looks a bit like a greenish-gray version of a Renegade. No doubt the rear hackle passes for the waving-tail appendages of a swimming damsel nymph.

It's a fish-eat-fish world out there. While rainbows can, under the right circumstances, acquire a taste for minnows, large brown trout can and often do indulge their taste for small rainbows.

A case in point is—or was, anyway—Dillon Reservoir on the Blue River, just on the west side of the Continental Divide about seventy miles due west of Denver. For many years after the filling of the reservoir in the mid-1960s, Dillon became a hotbed of trophy-class fishing for browns. The fishery has declined for a variety of reasons in the past several years, but there was a period in the 1970s and 1980s when knowledgeable anglers didn't consider a Dillon brown a real bruiser unless it reached about six pounds. Occasional ten- to twenty-pounders were taken over a twenty-year period.

Joe Butler Jr. of Denver acquired a reputation as a big-trout specialist partly based on his exploits at Dillon. He is also the holder of a world fly-fishing leader-class record (8-pound-test tippet) for browns, with a twenty-seven-pound, three-ounce fish taken at Flaming Gorge Reservoir in Utah in 1978. That fish, and many of the lesser but still impressive browns that he took at Dillon, fit a peculiar pattern that Butler put together over many seasons of fishing streamer flies and large floating-diving lures for big, reservoir-dwelling browns: They became vulnerable because they ventured into shallow water to feed on fingerling or "catchable-size" rainbow trout (eight to twelve inches) fresh off the hatchery truck.

Maybe you could call it a case of matching the hatchery.

Butler and his circle of lunker-hunting buddies used to read the newspapers and the regional hook-and-bullet magazines with a keen eye toward the state rainbow-trout stocking schedules. If Dillon Reservoir showed up on the list, they headed out Interstate 70 with every expectation of hooking at least one or two very large predatory browns in the shallow bay areas where the stock trucks dumped their loads. Their streamers were tied, or their lures painted, to look like small rainbow trout. The rest was just a matter of being there.

Minnows, damselflies, small stocker rainbows—those fit into the category of biological phenomena that can turn an apathetic population of mountain-reservoir fish into reckless predators. The other major factors are season and weather. Reservoir trout are most easily reached from shore or by wading anglers right after ice-out and right before ice-over. The unlocking of a winter-imprisoned lake sends trout cruising shoreline areas, either foraging or seeking spawning territory or both. This key period typically lasts two weeks to a month.

At Colorado's Spinney Mountain Reservoir on the South Platte drainage, large rainbows, cutthroats, and browns succumb to spoons, jigs, and flies such as the Woolly Bugger in the often arcticlike conditions that follow ice-out. If the wind's blowing, so much the better. The wind sends wave action crashing into the shoreline, which in turn shakes loose the crayfish, shrimp, and other delicacies that large trout love. In the fall, another orgy of near-shore feeding ensues in the last days of ice-free water, as if the trout know that a long, hard winter is impending and they better stock up.

Sometimes, though, the stimulation is purely meteorological on a short-term basis at any time of year. Walleye fishermen know they can depend on more consistent action when wind ruffles or whitecaps the surface of a lake—the hallowed "walleye chop"—and a change in the weather that brings wind can have much the same effect on the behavior of other reservoir fish, including trout, bass, and northern pike. Wind oxygenates a reservoir, creates a surface protective layer that gives prowling fish a sense of confidence, and concentrates forage on the side of the lake into which the wind is blowing. Anglers who stand with the wind at their backs so they can make long, effortless casts are often casting into fishless water.

Tarryall Reservoir is as placid as the surface of a mirror, which makes for an appealing, picture-postcard scene of pine-topped ridges reflected in the olive mirror of the lake. But it is also making for lousy pike fishing. The sum total of the efforts of three of us so far this day—and we are well into the afternoon—has been two smallish northerns. My two companions, who have accompanied me on this jaunt with some misgivings (Tarryall at that time was known as a trout lake, not a pike lake), finally walk over into the inviting coolness of the lakeside grass and sprawl out to take a nap.

But word has come to me in recent days that several pike in the four- to ten-pound class have been turning up on the lures of shocked trout trollers lately, and in one case, a shaken spin fisherman had come home muttering about toothy-jawed pike chomping down on his plastic casting bubble.

My partners are rudely awakened from their snooze by the patter of raindrops on their faces. A chill wind has swept in out of the west, riding the turmoil of a towering thunderhead. Suddenly, the stillness of flat water in the weedy bay becomes a wind-driven washboard of whitecaps. Almost as one, the three of us are back out in the water, double-hauling black streamer flies tied to forty-pound-shock tippets. This is purely a mountain-reservoir reflex on our part, grounded in years of trout fishing, not pike fishing.

But the effect is exactly the same: Pike that have been sulking in deeper water are suddenly up atop the shallow weed beds, prowling freely and hammering our streamer flies before we can strip them in more than a few feet. Within two hours, the windstorm has passed, but three limits of pike going five to eight pounds are on the stringer. We carry the stringer over to a dike, where a family fishing for trout has ventured back out from their nearby camper. We ask the man in the family to use one of our cameras to take a photo of us with our catch. The guy agrees, but first he stares down at the pile of pike and shakes his head in rueful amazement.

"You know," he says, "I drove all this way from Minnesota, where the lakes are full of pike, to fish for trout. And I end up at a lake where the locals are catching pike."

We commiserate. It is, after all, a reverse case of being there.

PART FOUR

PEOPLE,
PRIDE &
PREJUDICE

CHAPTER 12
Heavy Hitters

I CAUGHT MY FIRST TROUT WITH JOE BROOKS. WE WERE ON THE Big Hole River in southwestern Montana. The trout was a brown, and the year, if I remember correctly, was 1952. Actually, this took place only in the pages of *Outdoor Life* magazine—and in the fertile, vicarious environs of my young fisherman's imagination. As an avid reader, I made Brooks my hero and my mentor. In a make-believe sense, Brooks was the first famous fisherman I ever met or fished with. Much later, long after I actually did catch my first trout, I realized a boyhood dream. I became an outdoor writer and a fishing writer (or a writing fisher, if you consider that I was an angler first, before I was anything in a professional sense), just like my hero, Joe Brooks—well, sort of like him, anyway.

I don't put myself in anything close to Joe Brooks's league, but I do think that all outdoor writers, or fishing writers, must endure a degree of public misconception about just what it is they do or don't do. One misconception is that they don't work. They just accept gratuitous invitations to visit all sorts of outdoor shangri-las, where the fish and game are suicidal, and then when they get time, they make some money by telling less fortunate citizens how nice it was.

One example will serve. My boss at the newspaper was the sports editor. On one occasion, the sports-department secretary undertook to explain to him that my absence from the office one particular week was due to the fact that I was on vacation. To which the sports editor responded, "How can you tell?"

Ah, well, I have long since given up trying to enumerate for such skeptics the pressures and responsibilities of being a writer on outdoor subjects, one of which is actually functioning in the capacity of being a reporter. (No less a fishing-writer luminary and angling genius than A. J. McClane once told an effusive admirer, "All I am, really, is a reporter.")

In any case, I began to write stories and columns for the newspaper and for various magazines. And functioning as a reporter, it was my good fortune and pleasure to meet, interview, and occasionally fish with some of the finer and in several instances more famous fishermen in the land. Several come to mind—the late writer and filmmaker Lee Wulff; match-the-hatch master and author Ernest Schwiebert; the late Chuck Fothergill, Aspen-based guru of dead-drift nymphing; Jim Teeny, who concocted an unlikely looking nymph pattern and adapted it with fantastic success to steelhead and salmon fishing; the late Bill Phillipson, one of the West's great rod makers; the late Montana fly-shop owner Dan Bailey; Curt Gowdy, of sports broadcasting fame; Mike Lawson, of the Henry's Fork Anglers in Idaho; and the late fly-fishing author and Yellowstone-area expert Charlie Brooks, to name some of them.

In his confident, wise, insightful way, Wulff was perhaps the most impressive. He didn't stick to the well-worn paths of standard angling approaches. If ever there was a grand innovator in fly-fishing, Wulff was it. We owe to him, among other contributions, the wide acceptance of catch-and-release fishing, the invention of the fly vest, the use of lighter tackle, and the remarkably versatile line of Wulff flies.

Once, I attended a fly-fishing and casting school directed by Wulff and his wife, Joan. If anything, she cast better than he did, but that would be straining a comparison. He fished better than she did—in fact, better than almost anybody I ever saw fish with a fly rod. And that's not straining a comparison. The school was located by the Elk River, a small stream in northwestern Colorado. I attended in order to gather some story material and, I hoped, to add to my modest inventory of angling skills. I remember sitting on the bank with a group of students, watching Wulff demonstrate the art of using a skating-type dry fly to pound up trout when there was no hatch in progress. This is almost a lost art in today's match-the-hatch, numbers-oriented trout fishing. As he cast across a current glide and skittered his spider-style skater downstream and back across, he said, "And the trout should come up at about this point—" As if on cue, a two-pound rainbow appeared and slashed into the bouncing fly. Wulff barely seemed to look at the fish as he landed it while keeping up an instructive monologue.

Other famous anglers were equally enlightening. I spent two days on one trip to Montana fishing with Dan Bailey, the quiet, shy man who looked like an English professor but, as owner of the first major fly shop in the Livingston area, probably did more to bring fame to Montana trout fishing than any other individual (with the possible exception of Joe Brooks). This was somewhat of an irony, because Bailey, deep down, abhorred personal publicity and the possibility that he might be enticing unhealthy pressure to some of his beloved streams. But once, as we were discussing what was then a controversy about whether public access would continue to famed Armstrong Spring Creek, he told me, "Sometimes it takes publicity to save a stream for public fishing. You have to let the world know what it's in danger of losing."

It was on Armstrong when my head and ego puffed up with the satisfaction, on a windy afternoon, of actually out-fishing Bailey (if you consider total numbers of trout caught and released a measure of skill on a given day). The fact was, fishing tiny dry flies to selective trout in ultraclear currents was right up my alley—I had been doing it regularly on the challenging riffles and runs of my home river, the South Platte in Colorado.

The tables turned the next afternoon. Bailey drove me to a long, wide run on the brawling Yellowstone River in Paradise Valley, where sundown found us casting to a veritable horde of rising fish. Every time I cast my dry fly to a riser, I hooked a whitefish. Every time Bailey cast his to a riser, he hooked a brown trout. The largest for him that day, landed just as the last slanting rays of the setting sun dissolved on the ramparts of the Absaroka Mountains, was almost five pounds.

My hat size suddenly shrank a couple of notches and the air seeped out of my ego like a punctured tire. He had just caught and released a trout that would have been big enough to have its outline placed on his own shop's Wall of Fame—trout caught on Montana waters that weighed at least four pounds. The fact was that on big water, Bailey was light years ahead of me in casting and reading the water and in being able, in some way that was mysterious to me at that point, to tell a whitefish rise from a trout rise.

It also was my good fortune to have Chuck Fothergill, who championed the floating-line, weighted-leader approach to nymphing, instruct me on that technique when it was still an arcane way of fly-fishing to many anglers. After four or five trips with Fothergill on his beloved Roaring Fork River, my ratio of hookups to hours spent fishing soared exponentially.

I have done many interviews with famed fishermen, but the most memorable was with Ted Williams, the Boston Red Sox slugger who was the last man in major league baseball ever to hit for a season average over .400. I had just settled into a job as newspaper outdoor editor, and I was wet enough behind the ears to float a No. 8 Sofa Pillow. I knew a lot less about fishing then than I know now, but I knew that Williams, then manager of the Washington Senators American League team, was a highly skilled fly-fisherman, particularly in salt water and with Atlantic salmon.

He was in Denver with his team to play an exhibition game with the local minor-league farm team of the Senators. Somebody in the sports department told me where Williams and his players were staying. Unannounced, I drove over to the hotel to try to buttonhole Williams. I encountered him outside the hotel coffee shop. I walked up, told him I was from the *Denver Post*, and asked for an interview.

"Didn't you get the word?" he bellowed. "The press conference is at 2 P.M."

"I don't want to talk about baseball," I managed to say.

"What the hell do you want to talk about?" Williams said.

"Fishing," I said. "Fly-fishing."

His intent eyes—the eyes that reportedly could see the seams on a fast ball headed to the plate—suddenly sparkled. "Hell," he roared, "why didn't you say so? Let's get a cup of coffee."

Williams was an intimidating presence, with an aura around him that you normally associate with presidents or commanding generals—or maybe drill sergeants and large-bodied highway patrolmen. You didn't interview Ted Williams. You asked a question, and if it tweaked his imagination or interest, you got a lecture. I must have asked the right question, because before the coffee arrived, Teddy Ballgame was well into his sermon. The question, admittedly a leading one, was, "Which of all the game fish do you consider the most challenging?"

"The Atlantic salmon is the greatest game fish in the world!" Williams all but shouted, in tones Moses would have used to announce the commandments he brought down from the mountain. Heads at nearby tables swiveled in our direction.

The subject of Atlantic salmon led naturally, for Williams, into a speech about fly rods, fly-rod actions, and casting techniques. He then paused for a breath and asked me a question: "What kind of action do you prefer in a fly rod?"

I took this to be some sort of test. Hell, if I could make a forty-foot cast in those days without collapsing the loop or slapping line on the water, I didn't care what kind of action the rod had. This was before the advent of graphite rods. But I said, "I guess I prefer something closer to a slow action, a parabolic action, than a fast tip." And held my breath.

Williams frowned, then broke into a boyish grin. "Damn right!" he roared. "For most fishing, it will do the best job." Then Williams grabbed my pen and notebook and proceeded to diagram oscillations of various rod tapers. I had no idea what he was talking about, but I nodded enthusiastically. Now Williams not only was controlling the interview, he was recording it, too.

I finally got my notebook back. I'm not sure about the pen. But I know I left the hotel with plenty of column fodder, along with a promise that a Williams-autographed, glass fly rod (graphite was only a gleam in some rod-maker's eye) would be arriving in a few days from Sears Roebuck (Williams at that time endorsed a line of fishing tackle for Sears). It did arrive, and I used it for years.

These talents and personalities were awe-inspiring in their individual ways. Back toward the beginning of these reminiscences, I made the observation that Lee Wulff fished more skillfully than almost anybody I ever saw. The "almost" qualification may have seemed surprising to those who are familiar with the exploits of Wulff, who died in his eighties, at the controls of a light plane that crashed.

Actually, I didn't spend much time on the water with Lee Wulff, and the time I did spend was as a student and observer. But I have spent a lot of time on it with the man I think may be the finest fly-fisherman in the country—George Anderson, owner of the Yellowstone Angler shop in Livingston. I would often fly up to Bozeman, and George would meet me in one of his well-traveled, battered, foreign-made cars. We'd soon be off on a vagabond odyssey to the best waters that southwestern Montana and the Yellowstone National Park region had to offer—the Madison, the Yellowstone, the Firehole, the Lewis, the Henry's Fork of the Snake, and the Livingston-area spring creeks.

No one I ever fly-fished with did it with more modest, casual-looking efficiency and astounding success than Anderson. No one ever waded more boldly, either. George's tree-trunk legs can slosh him out into the powerful Madison with the imperviousness of a water buffalo. He could, and did, wade the Madison while hanging onto me with one arm so I wouldn't slip. And when George Anderson gets into casting position, he is a relentless, no-wasted-motion, angling predator. He often fishes with fly patterns he concocted himself—including the now-famous George's Rubber-Leg Stone, a woven-body stonefly nymph imitation. At least once, he used that pattern to take top honors in the Jackson, Wyoming, One Fly competition—whoever lands and releases the most trout on a single pattern wins. The competition is pretty fierce, too.

One day, Anderson showed me my first Woolly Bugger streamer fly, back when almost nobody had heard of it. That evening, he used it to hoodwink the selective rainbows of Nelson's Spring Creek, while I was struggling to match a hatch of midges. I should have paid attention—I didn't start using the pattern extensively until after it had become as common in fly-vest pockets as loose lint.

But I'll remember most the afternoon on the Henry's Fork, when George, stalking individual bank-sipping rainbows in the three- to five-pound class, plucked four of them in succession from a stretch of bank no more than fifteen feet long. He frequently switched flies, scoring with the second or third choice on three out of the four fish—going from a no-hackle mayfly pattern to a caddis pattern to a hackled mayfly pattern as if he could read not only the rise forms but the minds of the trout as well.

You can't help but learn from anglers such as these. And one of the lessons you learn, indelibly, is humility.

CHAPTER 13

COUNTING COUP

A MIDDLE-AGED WOMAN OF MY ACQUAINTANCE RECENTLY TOOK the plunge into fly-fishing. She even signed up for lessons. One of the sessions took place on the South Platte River, where the class learned, among other things, the basic points about casting. Among the instructions that stuck in her mind was this one: "Forget that stuff you saw in *A River Runs Through It*," the instructor said. "That isn't really how it works."

I had to chuckle at that. The Robert Redford–directed movie based on the late Norman Maclean's wonderful, haunting novella probably has brought more people into fly-fishing in the past several years (including women) than ventured into the sport in the previous thirty. This can be viewed as something of an irony. There are large differences between today's trout fishing and the fishing Norman Maclean and his father and brother enjoyed sixty or more years ago on the prime waters of western Montana. In Redford's movie, the spectacular, somewhat hokey visual images that Hollywood is so clever at creating bear only a superficial resemblance to today's realities.

Casting is just one example. In the movie, you see strong young men waving bamboo rods in repetitive arcs, apparently carrying sixty feet of fly line in the air across fast, heavy, conflicting currents and then shooting twenty more feet of line in what look to be routine, eighty-foot casts. And then, wonder of wonders, with all that line on the water, they manage to set the hook into a slab-sided trout! Few people can cast a fly line eighty feet, even with today's marvelous and easier-to-use graphite rods. Most hook setting is done at ranges much closer to twenty-five feet than eighty, and the hard-pressured, selective trout on many of the best streams today respond not to bulky, floating concoctions on the surface, but to tiny nymphs dead-drifted near bottom or equally tiny floating flies.

In truth, Maclean's masterpiece was much more a story about a brother's love for a wayward brother than it was about fly-fishing in Montana. The fishing and the river were the vehicles by which the author brought the reader to the basic truth that you cannot control the destinies of others, no matter how much you love them. In the end, you simply are left to cherish the good moments that you shared with them.

Some other incongruities come to mind in the phenomenon surrounding the movie adaptation of *A River Runs Through It*. Ask any fly-shop owner, and he'll tell you how much the movie did for his business. But was it an honest portrayal of fly-fishing as we know it? Of course not, partly for the reasons already enumerated. But it may have been an honest portrayal of fly-fishing as our predecessors knew it in the first four decades of this century. Many of the Macleans' fishing adventures took place on the Big Blackfoot River, which, in recent years, has been largely a polluted, silted, dewatered shadow of its former self (although there are successful efforts being made to restore it).

And killing your limit of trout is no longer a widely accepted goal, or even a legal possibility, on most major rivers. In the halcyon years the Macleans enjoyed, there were so few really competent anglers prowling the fine rivers of Montana and other western states that these waters could afford what are now considered shockingly liberal limits. The average-size wicker creel—and everybody carried one—was strained to hold a day's catch. The limit in the 1930s in Montana was probably twenty trout. The concept of catching trout just to release them was as remote from everyday thinking as the notion that mankind would someday set foot on the moon. This does not make the anglers of those years reprehensible—it just reflects the differences in eras. Today, a fly-fisherman walking around with a wicker basket would be presumed to be carrying his lunch and a bottle of wine in it.

A reading of the book shows that Norman Maclean and his brother, Paul, had a kind of sibling rivalry going every time they waded into a river. To them, you didn't experience a totally successful day, and you failed to prove your prowess as a fly-fisherman and your masculinity as a kind of hunter/provider, if you didn't "get your limit." There are still some old-timers around who think in these terms, but they are anomalies, and their numbers dwindle inexorably.

The Maclean brothers weren't what one friend of mine terms "bean counters"—anglers who keep score based on numbers of fish caught and released. Norman and Paul were carcass counters. When there was a limit of trout in their baskets, they stopped fishing. Today, there are bean counters—or, if you prefer, scorekeepers. It's interesting to examine the question of which of the two types of counters—carcass or bean—can lay claim to the moral high ground. Or, if either can. Ask a bean counter how the fishing went for him on a given day, and he most likely *won't* say something like, "It was great—the trout were tearing up a caddis emerger fished down and across." What he *will* say is, "I took twenty-four trout going twelve to twenty inches." The measure of a rewarding day, to him, is the tally at the bottom of the ledger sheet.

A highly skilled and noted fisherman once gave a seminar on trout fishing. In the "news release" announcing the subject matter, time, and place of the seminar, this angler was described as once having caught and released more than 200 trout averaging five pounds in one area in a few days, during a time when large rainbows and cutthroats were making spawning runs into reservoir tributaries. There is no question that this guy is a remarkably talented angler—one of the best in the country. And maybe whoever wrote the release, if the angler himself didn't, just got their figures screwed up. But for the hell of it, I put my pencil to the reported numbers of caught fish, in the context of hours of fishing time available in the day and the number of days in which he was said to have accomplished this staggering feat. And what I came up with is the mathematical fact that he would have had to land and release, as an average, a five-pound trout approximately every ten minutes. This is taking into account probable travel time and length of daylight each day. My ten-minute calculation didn't allow any time for much else but wading, casting, setting the hook, fighting the fish, and turning it loose. The angler would have had little or no time for playing and losing a fish, or for an occasional pause to expel bodily wastes. (Hell, who knows—maybe he pissed in his waders.) He would have had to eat lunch with a sandwich in one hand and a fly rod in the other.

Even if you accept that he did all this, you are finally left with the perplexing questions of what he was trying to prove, and why he felt the need to prove it.

This, of course, is an extreme example of what has happened with some modern-day fishermen. But these guys approach fishing much the same way affluent buyers approach an auction—whoever comes up with the biggest number walks away with the prize. Alas, these types often are unquestionably skilled anglers. There is no law of physics or human nature that says a braggart can't be telling at least a measure of the truth. Most of them are also very boring to be around—they never stop telling you how good they are or instructing you on how you can get to be almost as good. (Maybe there's some jealousy and envy involved in this perception; I am certainly willing to concede that possibility.) Sometimes they strike me as being modern-day throwbacks to the old western gunfighter, constantly having to reestablish his reputation.

These guys are in a class that writer Tom McGuane describes as being uncomfortable with the prospect of leisure for its own sake. To them, leisure is sinful if it is not linked to some tangible accumulation. Ironically, their propensity to strive for and later proclaim outlandish scores is partly made possible by low-kill and no-kill regulations. These regulations keep the better trout in the water and are critical to the future of trout fishing. With today's angling pressure, restrictive regulations are all that stand between anglers and troutless rivers. But I don't think they were meant to turn fishing into a scorekeeping contest.

In the days of the Macleans, trout fishing accommodated a part of human nature that harbors a kind of caveman, self-provider instinct. Now, when you embrace the very necessary (on some waters) catch-and-release concept, you are rejecting the caveman part—the part that derives satisfaction, purpose, and self-esteem from being skilled enough to catch and kill a fish or a few fish for the dinner table. But if you reject (quite appropriately in these times) that instinct, something must take its place. And unfortunately, what tends to take its place on the best catch-and-release waters is an ego-massaging, scorekeeping mentality—a numbers game—bean counting, if you will. You can't bring home the bacon, so you bring home the beans. Or, to look at it another way, you are indulging a modern-day version of the old Indian practice of "counting coup"—tagging or touching an enemy, or stealing something from the enemy, without actually doing any killing.

If the limit were four fish, or two, the angler would leave the water when he or she creeled four, or two, and the spouse, kiddies, or whoever else was waiting at home at the end of the day would recognize this tangible success and offer congratulations on it. In a sense, that scenario can be viewed as more ethical than stopping fishing after twenty-four trout have been caught and released. There are those who don't fish and who view this as harassing twenty-four trout to satisfy some personal notion of what constitutes a triumphant and productive day. For that matter, there are some who *do* fish and view it that way.

I am not one of those—not exactly, anyway. There are days (occasional, to be sure) when I really have things going on a stream or lake, when I'm on a roll, and after releasing yet another fish, it suddenly dawns on me that even if I haven't been keeping a precise count, I'm playing the numbers game—counting coup, if you will. I could have quit earlier and hooked, landed, and handled fewer trout.

On the other hand, one way to look at this is to concede that, after all, the main object of this game called fishing is to have fun catching fish. Thus, the more you catch, the more fun you have. But I'm getting a bit disenchanted with the arbitrary notion that the higher the number, the better the fisherman. Such a conclusion implies that there can't be a skilled angler who *chooses* to quit fishing while the fish are still biting, or who takes his time between fish. I am equally disenchanted with complaints from some of the bean-counter set that too many of these trout they're catching (and counting) are pathetic because they have scars, sores, torn jaws, and missing gill plates.

Sorry, guys. You can't have it both ways. Can you honestly expect to exercise the same group of trout on the end of a hook and line day after day after day and not expect them to show signs of the strain? I don't think so. It seems fairly obvious that what you and I can do is subtract some of the competitive, ego-driven scorekeeping from a day spent on the water, particularly on catch-and-release water. You can be satisfied with fewer hookups. You can quit at fifteen, or ten, or even eight or six, instead of twenty-four or thirty-three or whatever.

You can also dispense with the notion, or the implication, that releasing a trout or other fish is by definition a noble act—one that everyone should emulate at all times or else suffer the stigma of being branded an unfeeling brute. It seems to me that releasing a fish is prudent, caring, sensitive, and often necessary in the context of the conservation and maintenance of many fisheries. But noble—no. This is probably straining for an analogy, but why is releasing a hooked fish any more noble than terrorizing somebody by pointing a gun at him for a period of time, then saying, "I've decided not to shoot you?" Or at least, if the act of releasing a fish does involve some small degree of nobility, that nobility certainly isn't multiplied by the number of times the act is repeated in a day of fishing. If anything, the more times it is repeated, the less noble it becomes.

What you can do, in addition, is make sure that you don't handle the trout any more than necessary, and handle it carefully when you do. You can keep it in the water during the handling and the removal of the hook—preferably one that is barbless—and get the fish swimming again as quickly as possible. You can use the strongest leader tippets that are possible to fool the fish with so as to land them sooner and not play them to exhaustion.

Or, you can fish somewhere else, in waters that are under less pressure, where it's still within the regulations and compatible with the resource to kill a few trout and take them home to eat. They may not be as big as those in catch-and-release waters, but chances are they won't have any hook scars, either. And if you quit when you creel your limit, you won't need a calculator to tally up the numbers.

If fly-fishing for trout becomes a numbers game, something far more precious has been lost than the quality of fishing the Maclean brothers enjoyed six decades ago.

Chapter 14

"My way or the highway"

It is said by many that the ultimate angling experience is taking a saltwater permit on a fly. Others argue for the bonefish, the tarpon, or the Atlantic salmon. Some say steelhead. Still others define the issue in meticulous detail, saying the ultimate is hooking and landing something on the order of an eight-pound brown trout on a No. 24 dry fly, on 7X leader (possibly with one hand tied behind your back). Although such subjective judgments are based in part on the fish's difficulty of capture with the method of choice, it's not the only criterion. If it were, taking a bullhead catfish (or maybe a flounder) on a dry fly would be the ultimate.

The prevailing guideline is the angler's perception of the species itself—its beauty, size, strength, speed, elusiveness, and character, to the extent a fish can be said to have character. (And a thirty-pound permit, nosing up to your creatively tied, perfectly presented, crab-imitation fly and then turning that nose up to swim away—well, such a fish can definitely be said to have character.) So there are permit and bonefish connoisseurs, salmon fanciers, steelhead junkies, bass fanatics, walleye weirdos, muskie maniacs, and so forth. They all share this much in common—they are species oriented and, to some degree, method fixated.

This sort of stuff can make for magnificent obsessions and fertile fodder for debate—until it gets to the point where the species advocacy becomes as myopic as an armadillo with a cataract problem. Not that preferring one species or method of fishing over another is unnatural—it's just as human as preferring football over baseball or filet mignon over fried chicken. But it seems sort of silly to refuse to watch baseball when football's not in season, or to turn down a plate of fried chicken because a steak doesn't happen to be available at the time. To move it out of the realm of metaphor, if I am a true angler, captivated by the sport itself, as I most certainly am, I am not going to refuse to fish for striped bass because there aren't any steelhead around, or decline to use sunken nymphs if the trout aren't at the surface taking dry flies. To do so, to me, would be foolishly self-defeating. I like to catch fish too much. But I would be short-sighted if I failed to appreciate somebody else's love, fascination, and concern for their favored sport fish and preferred method. Live and let fish, I say.

Unfortunately, there is not always a spirit of unity and tolerance among anglers. For example, a friend of mine who spends 95 percent of his fishing time pursuing largemouth bass, smallmouth bass, and walleyes—and doing it with expert proficiency—has bitter feelings toward Trout Unlimited, the trout-conservation organization. He resents the influence Trout Unlimited has, or that he perceives it has, over Colorado's fish-management affairs.

"Trout aren't the only fish in the water," he grumps. "Trout Unlimited wants everybody to support them in protecting trout streams, but where were they when we lost a whole lake full of warm-water fish when the irrigation people drained (here he named a popular Front Range reservoir)?"

Well, maybe the same place the bass clubs were when Trout Unlimited was arguing a few years back that whirling disease really *was* a threat to rainbow trout populations—and very few people were listening. Now, the state-fisheries authorities find themselves struggling to save declining populations of wild rainbows and are spending millions of dollars to clean up hatcheries and to do whirling-disease research. Yet they are falling woefully short of the number of "clean fish" needed for stocking mountain reservoirs and high-country lakes. Those millions of dollars come out of the same pot that contains the money my bass-fishing friend spent for his fishing license. Realistically, every decline in a particular fishery is a loss to fishing in general. In other words, don't ask for whom the bell tolls.

Species advocacy is fine and even admirable when the advocate puts his personal commitment and money where his fascination is. But it shouldn't be carried to the extreme where nothing else in the world of fisheries matters, and when the advocate is so intensely focused that he distrusts even the professional fish biologists who are, after all, only trying to help him and the species he worships. (Debating the wisdom of their management decisions is one thing; believing them to be conniving liars is something else.)

In my years as the *Denver Post*'s outdoor editor, I got countless calls and letters from anglers taking issue with some aspect or other of the fish-management decisions of the Colorado Division of Wildlife. Sometimes, I agreed with them. Other times, their positions were ill thought-out and even childish.

One of the classics in that genre was a fellow who happened to be a lake-trout (aka mackinaw trout) fanatic. All in the same week, I received three telephone calls and one letter from this reader, who concentrates on Colorado's Lake Granby for his lake-trout fishing. He was outraged by a report in the *Denver Post* about a Colorado Division of Wildlife lake-trout study at Granby. The study centered on hooking mortality with Granby lakers. It found that almost nine out of ten lake trout caught from deep water and released in the summer months at Granby die anyway—from the trauma of the changing pressures as they are hauled up, as well as from the impact of water-temperature changes and less-than-careful handling.

The biologists reasoned that the only sensible thing to do was liberalize the lake-trout creel limit during those summer months, because if a lake trout was going to be a dead fish anyway, its death may as well serve some useful purpose for the angler. If you believe the research findings, that rationale is hard to argue with. (Then again, you can argue that no fish is going to survive if it's reclining in somebody's ice chest.)

The angry reader saw this management decision as a conspiracy to get rid of lake trout at Granby in order to restore it to its former status as a first-class kokanee-salmon lake. First of all, if this reader knew his Lake Granby history, he should have known that if any population of fish in the state of Colorado has received exceptional hands-on care and protection, to the point of micromanaging, it is the Granby lake-trout population. The lake's chief biologist, who watches over these fish with the protective intensity of a mother goose leading a troop of goslings, would allow the destruction of his beloved mackinaws only over his dead body.

And while lake trout certainly do function as predators foraging on the smaller salmon (and trout) at times, the main reason for the decline of kokanees at Granby was the stocking many years ago of mysis shrimp in the lake. This was intended as a move to give the lake trout and other fish something new to munch on, but the mysis consumed most of the plankton on which the kokanee salmon depend for food. (This was certainly a management decision that, in retrospect, was a real screw-up—if you prefer trolling for kokanees or rainbows over deep-jigging for lake trout.) The point is, even if all the lakers disappeared, it's unlikely that Granby would revert to a premier kokanee fishery.

I have absolutely nothing against either kokanee salmon or lake trout. I have spent many enjoyable days on reservoirs trolling for kokanees, fly-fishing for them when they're on stream-spawning runs, and jigging for them through the ice. Other days have been spent jigging or casting for lake trout at Granby, and one of my more cherished memories is of landing an eighteen-pound Granby laker on light spinning tackle and a quarter-ounce jig. This fish was taken from the currents of the south fork of the Colorado River at least a mile above its inlet into Lake Granby, which makes the fish and the memory even more special.

But it is my conviction that, regardless of the species in question, there is a tendency toward narrow-mindedness in overzealous, species-based activism, whether individual in nature or organized.

Not long ago, I read a newspaper story—one of those in-depth "think" pieces that conservation writers like to develop. It presented a pretty convincing case that organized advocacy groups in the sport of fishing are turning it into a fragmented, tribal battlefield over species-oriented issues—trout fishermen versus walleye fishermen, largemouth bass enthusiasts versus striped-bass anglers, trout fishermen versus northern pike fanciers, and so forth.

The reporter in this story noted that there are many species-devoted organizations in this country now, from Trout Unlimited to Bass Anglers Sportsman Society to Walleyes Unlimited to Muskies Inc. to the Striped Bass Association, and so on. His story painted a potentially dark picture for the future of fishing. The fear expressed in this case was that in their zeal to promote their own particular offshoots of the sport, these groups are endangering the overall resources. There were references to walleyes and northern pike being stocked illegally in trout waters (a very real concern in some western states) and to the complaints of largemouth bass and crappie fishermen, who believe introductions of stripers are devastating the smaller species in some reservoirs. (Biologists generally maintain that this particular fear is unfounded, because adult stripers don't spend much time in shallow or relatively shallow areas, while largemouths and crappies do.)

I think there is some cause for worry in all of this, but not necessarily because of any widespread, direct, competitive threat to certain fish by other fish. Rather, I suspect the main threat is to participation in the sport of angling itself—and, therefore, it's an indirect threat to the future welfare of *all* fish and their habitat.

There is, in my opinion, a possibility that overall numbers of anglers will dwindle if fish management sinks to the level of a constant shouting match between advocates of certain species. Or worse, it will become a confused mishmash of "bucket biology"—with misguided, angry anglers out dumping their favorite sport fish in any water they choose.

Although the ranks of fly-fishermen have grown in the past two decades, the percentage of anglers in general is beginning to shrink a bit in proportion to the growth of the U.S. population. This is probably a reflection of the urbanization of America, but it also may reflect disenchantment by anglers who simply decide not to buy a license again. They are put off when they hear constant, strident, mindless complaining about how a particular species is being managed. This sort of disenchantment doesn't help sustain or increase the backbone of the rank-and-file, license-buying public.

The fact is, the fishing world doesn't revolve around whatever species you or I care to lionize. My, or your, personal part of that world might revolve around trout, or salmon, or bass, or walleyes, or whatever, but fishing as a whole does not. Rather, the world of sport fishing and its management revolves around a large, core group of millions of men, women, and youngsters who are willing to put up their cash to buy licenses and fishing equipment (regardless of what they choose to fish for and the tackle they prefer). The license revenue and the taxes on that equipment are utilized by state and federal agencies to make sure all of us get our chance at healthy populations of fish in protected habitat.

Most of these license buyers are not professionals, nor do they aspire to be. They don't compete in tournaments. They don't belong to any angling organization or beat the drums for any particular species of fish. They may use bait, they may use lures, they may use flies—or maybe all three at various times—and they just enjoy going fishing, are thrilled if they catch something, and are doubly delighted if they get to keep a few legal-size fish for supper, assuming the regulations allow it. Many of them are bored and put off by what must seem to be highly subjective and convoluted debates about what regulations are best for what species at what stream or lake.

Instead of being denigrated, they should be allowed to share in the conservation-minded approaches; they ought to be offered reasons why a given stream needs a no-kill rule or a given lake needs a size minimum on lake trout. If these people are lost, the financial and demographic foundation of sport fishing and fish management is also lost. It makes sense that they should be enlisted and educated on conservation issues, not belittled or ignored.

Rest assured that, if a significant percentage of this core group defects from the ranks, the financial slack would not be taken up by the pompous protectors of all animal and fish life, such as People for the Ethical Treatment of Animals—which has "declared war on fishing." They would continue to transport their membership money to the bank, and I doubt they would make a donation stop at the nearest office of the fish and game department on the way.

Here are just a couple of examples of how the average angler sometimes gets lost in the regulatory, species-advocacy shuffle. Whatever you may think about the walleye regulations in Colorado, the rather complex, conservative creel limits on this species (depending on the river drainage or the individual reservoir) are the result of intense lobbying by the Colorado Walleye Association. The most influential anglers in this group are tournament anglers, who don't see a walleye as the most delicious fish that ever graced a frying pan, but rather as another notch in the tournament scorekeeping that leads either to a cash (or merchandise) prize, a trophy, or both. They release all their fish in their tournaments, which is admirable and maybe even necessary in the intense, finely skilled angling pressure that tournaments generate. But these anglers don't reflect the reality of the average fisherman out on a weekend trying to catch a few walleyes.

Colorado fish managers a few years ago proposed to slightly liberalize and generalize walleye limits so that the whole walleye-regulation picture would be more uniform. The walleye association put the quash on this in a hurry, lobbying in favor of a confusing variety of limits and size restrictions, depending on the lake. And that's what they, and the rest of us, got.

You can argue that this is the smart way to go, or you can argue it isn't. There are reasonable rationales on both sides of the argument. But if you do much traveling as a walleye angler, you better have the regulations brochure in your tackle box, lest you put a sixteen-incher in the live-well when the lake minimum-size limit is confined to eighteen-inchers. Go to one lake and the limit is four walleyes; go to another one and it's five; go to yet another and it's ten. This is pretty esoteric regulatory stuff for a fish that generally doesn't fight well, wouldn't exist at all in Colorado if not for annual stocking operations (again, paid for by *all* license buyers), and, as suggested earlier, reaches the zenith of its considerable value as a sport fish when it is coated in cornmeal and sizzling in oil.

Lest any walleye afficionados misinterpret my remarks and come calling with lynch ropes, let me hurriedly add the disclaimer—I believe small walleyes should be released. I consider the catching of truly big walleyes (which can be damned elusive) to be one of the more intriguing challenges in angling. I don't devote a lot of space on my family-room walls to mounted fish (there are four in all), but I have a spot of honor now occupied by an eleven-pound walleye taken by wading and casting at Cherry Creek Reservoir.

I have released my share of walleyes and eaten my share, but I don't think this particular species, however much I esteem it, qualifies as anything approaching a mandatory catch-and-release quarry. That's essentially what it becomes, for most anglers, when you place an eighteen-inch minimum on a given lake in Colorado.

Then there was the time that Colorado Trout Unlimited raised hell about the state wildlife agency's decision to issue eighty special tags in a drawing to anglers who might want to kill a trophy rainbow trout in the South Platte between the Elevenmile Reservoir inlet and Spinney Mountain Dam. It is not uncommon to find five- to ten-pounders making spawning runs up this stretch in the spring out of Elevenmile.

You would have thought, judging by the reaction from Trout Unlimited members, that somebody had suggested selling their children to slave traders. Apparently, it did not occur to them that the removal of eighty rainbow trout out of a population made possible by the stocking of hundreds of thousands of fingerlings would be equivalent to taking a spoonful of sand out of a sandbox. Or if it did occur to them, they didn't care; it was, in their minds, wrong to kill any trout—"trophy" fish especially.

If they had argued that maintaining a total no-kill rule on this three miles of river (which is what the regulation now says) would be in the best interest of regulatory uniformity, and that trout spawners should be allowed to spawn, they would have had a more cogent and acceptable argument.

Instead, they made it sound as if anybody who desired to kill a large trout in the last year or two of its life was a thoughtless cretin. This stance, though it eventually prevailed, probably did more to alienate nonaffiliated anglers from the admirable goals of Trout Unlimited than any other position Colorado Trout Unlimited ever took.

And before you Trout Unlimited folks tighten up the hangman's knots on your lynch ropes, let me hasten to add—I have never killed a trout on the Spinney Mountain section of the South Platte, even when it was legal to do so. And I believe Trout Unlimited has done more to conserve the wonderful cold-water fish resources of America than any other single organization or segment of our society. Trout Unlimited was at the forefront of habitat-improvement and conservation efforts, and limited-kill regulations, back when those positions were generally viewed as the radical notions of a minority of self-centered elitists. A few years ago, when I had the feeling (probably paranoid) that I was a lone voice crying in the wilderness of the impending disaster of widespread whirling-disease devastation in Colorado, Trout Unlimited gave me unqualified support. For that, I am grateful, because I can remember a time when there were almost no such organized voices in any aspect of Colorado fish management.

Therefore, species-related conservation efforts definitely are important in fish management. Sometimes they are all that exist to prevent damage to, or the loss of, a particular fishery. There is simply a tendency at times to focus on the trees of sport fishing at the expense of the entire forest, or to toss the baby out with the bath water, or to do what could be summarized by whatever metaphor you think might fit.

Beyond the prejudicial tendency toward myopia that can be caused by species advocacy, there is the kind of prejudice that comes with fishing-method fixation. A fly-fisherman may look down his Polaroids at spin-fishermen. The dry-fly fanatic often takes a dim view of the nymph-fishing specialist. Fly- and lure-fishermen together may sneer at bait-fishermen. Float tubers think trollers are a menace. That sort of thing.

As noted elsewhere in these musings, it is my conviction that ethics, sportsmanship, and conservation are in the man, not the method, as long as the method fits with the regulations and the limits of the resource. I have no resentment of the fly-fisherman who has a problem with taking trout on, let's say, a dead-drifted stonefly nymph, as opposed to taking one on a floating fly. Where we part company is when he insists that *I* ought to have a problem with it.

The only place where I feel I might stray across a personal, live-and-let-live, fish-and-let-fish, philosophical line of thought in regard to choice of method is in the area of snagging. I don't believe, even if the regulations allow it and the resource can stand it, that snagging of species such as kokanee salmon remotely resembles any form of ethical, sporting, conservation-minding angling.

But sometimes I catch myself being a kind of purist in reverse. I dearly love to take trout on dry flies, but that doesn't diminish my enjoyment of taking them on dead-drift nymphs, no matter how many purists may equate nymphing with bait-dunking. Nor does having a taste for steak, as I said earlier, lessen my enjoyment of a bucket of fried chicken. I consider myself a fairly skilled nymph fisherman, and I get defensive about this at times, I guess.

One time, a fly-fishing friend of mine (a professional guide who is highly skilled at nymph fishing) joined up with me and a dry-fly fishing fanatic for a day on the South Platte at Deckers. This dry-fly advocate—and he is truly adept at stalking and hooking trout on floating flies—tends to think that nymph fishing in general (and use of the San Juan Worm in particular) is equivalent to admitting that catching trout, period, is more important to the angler than doing it in a graceful, artistic way. He is not particularly strident about this, but if you ask him, he'll tell you.

The day we hit the Platte at Deckers, the river was high and somewhat roily and the insect hatches were notable by their scarcity. After a couple of hours of probing the currents, it was obvious to all three of us that any trout that were going to be caught this day were going to be caught below the surface. My guide friend and I ended up hooking several nice trout on San Juan Worms and various midge-larva imitations, while the third member of our little group stuck faithfully to his unproductive (on this occasion) dry flies.

I found myself, back at the vehicle, with the three of us sipping beers toward the end of the day, rubbing it in with the dry-fly guy. ("Uh, how many fish did you say you hooked, Roger?") He took it good-naturedly, but it occurred to me suddenly that I was getting more than a friendly, playful measure of satisfaction out of dispensing the needle at his expense. It felt, guiltily, like a kind of reverse prejudice. Instead of needling him, I should have been admiring him for sticking to his principles. He had delivered no lectures or sermons (as I have done in this chapter); he was merely following the directions of his own angling philosophy. After all, you are the judge of the elements of your pleasure in fishing, and if it gives you more pleasure to catch fish with one approach than with another, why not please yourself to the utmost? Indeed, if that approach is so pleasing that you don't mind getting skunked when it doesn't work, as opposed to switching to something that does, what the hell? Who should object? Nobody, really.

As long as we take that stance and still maintain our bond as anglers, and as long as we unite in our mutual concern for all angling resources, we will be all right. So will the fish.

End of sermon. May the congregation go in peace. Now, can anybody give me any real insight on how to catch a bullhead on a dry fly?

special FISH special places

part FIVE

CHAPTER 15

THE GRACEFUL GRAYLING

IT IS NOT EASY TO HAVE A LOVE AFFAIR WHEN THE OBJECT OF your affection only makes an appearance in your life at intermittent and sometimes unpredictable times. But I suppose it would be accurate to say that I have had a fisherman's on-again, off-again love affair with the Arctic grayling.

Drawing out the analogy, the grayling has come into my angling life with the spontaneousness of an old girlfriend who peripatetically shows up in widely diverse places and demonstrates that the flame still burns brightly on both sides of the relationship. (I wish to make it clear to friends, family, and spouse that I have no such old girlfriend. This metaphor springs purely from imagination.) But my flings with the grayling have been very real and always rewarding.

My first encounter came in, of all places, the upper Green River in Wyoming, under the shadows of the Wind River Range. Three of us had decided to find out how big and how numerous the rainbow trout were on the stretch below Green River Lakes by making about a sixteen-mile float in a rubber raft, camping one night along the way. We had an assortment of tackle, including fly rods and ultralight spinning rods, thinking that if hatches were sparse or these trout somehow turned out to be cannibalistic fish-eaters, we would solve that problem with small spoons and spinners.

The first major revelation was that the Green River below the lakes is very slow moving. There are stretches you paddle through as if crossing a reservoir. This gets to be work, particularly when the wind blows upstream and it rains, which is what happened about half the time on the float. The second was that if there were any sizable, wild rainbows (or browns) in this section, they were notable by their shyness on this occasion. The rainbows we caught were small, suspiciously pale specimens that had the equally suspicious characteristic of hanging around the scattered campgrounds and road-access points along the way. Short of seeing them fall out of the hatchery truck, there was no way to prove they were stockers, but. . . . Third, most of the fish that chose to rise to our dry flies on this July adventure were whitefish, not trout. They got to be something of a nuisance, and they weren't very big, either.

It was a weird trip. Once, we came languishing around a bend in another slow, sweeping stretch through a grassy valley when there suddenly appeared before us an entire village of huge Indian tepees. They were crafted out of slender lodgepole pine logs and it felt eerily as if we had suddenly been transported in a time warp back to the mid-nineteenth century. I half-expected a fierce-looking brave to wander out of the bushes and offer to trade beaver pelts for a box of trout flies. As it turned out, the occupants weren't Sioux or Pawnee, but young people taking part in an Outward Bound exercise. We pulled out and visited awhile, and one of the counselors mentioned that he had seen "a whole bunch of fish" rising to some sort of hatch just downstream.

More whitefish, we thought, pushing back off in the raft a few minutes later. But as we floated around the next bend, I decided that when in Rome, you take what the Romans put on the menu, and I picked up my fly rod to make a cast with a small Adams pattern into the midst of a pocket of bankside risers. Nothing happened until the fly began to drag, and suddenly something pounced on it with a slashing lunge. This struck me as peculiar whitefish behavior, but it wasn't until the "whitefish" came out in a graceful jump that it dawned on me this was something entirely different. I was happily stunned when what came to raftside was a thirteen-inch grayling.

"Are there supposed to be grayling in this river?" I asked the Wyoming resident who was acting as our guide and chief rainshower-rower.

"I didn't think so,"he said, shaking his head.

This fish was not alone. We beached the raft and took wading stations along the run and in short order were periodically hooking twelve to fourteen-inch grayling with all the regularity of casting to rainbows rising to a mayfly hatch. The sleek fish with the saillike dorsals were feeding on midges but would accept any reasonable imitation of a gray or dark-colored insect no matter how it was presented.

I didn't learn a hell of a lot about grayling on that trip, other than that they existed somehow in the upper Green, and when they were hungry, it didn't take an angling wizard to catch one. That float occurred way back in the early 1970s. I don't know that grayling can still be found in the Green, but my semieducated guess, given the fact of their disappearance from most of their native waters in the contiguous states, is that they can't. There are remnant populations in Montana's Big Hole and Madison rivers. They also can be found in scattered lakes in Montana, certain lakes in Yellowstone National Park, and in isolated spots in other parts of Wyoming, Utah, and Colorado, most of those populations created or sustained by intermittent stocking.

The first installment of my advanced grayling education came on a wilderness lake in northern Saskatchewan. Ironically again, this was not a place where I had gone to fish for grayling, either.

I was in a commercially outfitted, backcountry camp consisting of tents with wooden floors on a bay of one of those myriad wilderness waters that sparkle in the green forests and tundra of the upper part of the province. The two chief attractions in the lake were unsophisticated northern pike and walleyes, both of which fully satisfied the piscatorial predilections of my tentmates, who happened to be a group of guys from Iowa. They had flown in by float plane one day ahead of my flight. They used spinning rods and bait-casting rods, their favorite lure was the Jack O' Diamonds spoon (which in some minds could replace the maple leaf as the Canadian national emblem), and their ultimate objective was to carry back to Des

Moines as much dry-iced poundage in fillets as the regulations and the float-plane weight capacity would allow.

After the third day, I tired somewhat of the pike-walleye routine, even after taking many of them on a fly rod. As we sat idly around camp one evening, watching an occasional lake whitefish sipping midges off the surface, I asked one of my guides—Colorado college kids freelancing with questionable legality as Canadian guides during the summer—whether the lake held any grayling.

"I've never caught 'em in the lake," he said. "But I've seen 'em at the outlet."

"The outlet?"

"Yeah, I've seen 'em where the river flows out on its way to the next lake," he said.

"The river" was the Geikie River. I didn't know it then, but the Geikie was considered one of Saskatchewan's premier grayling rivers. The outfitter hadn't even mentioned grayling in his description of the area's fishing possibilities. (After all, it's hard to fill a dry-ice crate with grayling fillets.)

"Can we fish it?"

"Sure," the kid shrugged. "We'll check it out in the morning if you want. It won't take long to get there in a canoe."

What I discovered at the outlet was a wide, sweeping expanse of pocket water gliding over submerged boulders, and down amongst the boulders were incredibly thick schools of grayling that looked like they weighed anywhere from a pound to three pounds. They wavered there in the clear current like small, sunken sailboats.

Ten minutes of casting a dry fly resulted in nothing. Twenty more minutes of dead-drifting a weighted nymph produced precisely one grayling—a fish of about a pound and a half. Reverting to my Ernie Schwiebert mode, which I call up like a faithful genie in times of desperation, I put the fly rod down and poked around in the shallows like a myopic shorebird. I dredged up a mossy stick and found it covered with stick-case caddis larva, and a dissection of one case revealed the brightest green worm, tiny though it was, I had ever seen.

I rummaged through a fly box and found a size 16 green-bodied caddis-larva imitation. I tied it on and dead-drifted it through the forest of dorsal fins. Still nothing. Deciding that the only thing to do, until something brilliant occurred to me, was to relax, I pulled a cigar out of my shirt pocket. I stuck it in my mouth, made yet another upstream, dead-drift-type cast with the floating line and slightly weighted leader, and clamped the rod under my arm to light the cigar after the drift played out below me and the line began to drag. The drag was pulling the little caddis pattern up toward the surface.

I won't say the rod was jerked out of my armpit, but there was a solid jolt, and when I looked, I saw the remnant of a splash where a grayling had risen to pounce on what the fish must have taken for a caddis emerger. This was a two-pounder, gleaming with the subtleties of a silver, gold, and turquoise body, and pale lavender spotting on a garish fan of a dorsal fin, all of which captivated me for a moment before I unhooked and released the fish. The stubborn fight had taken longer than I expected.

Some experienced anglers maintain that the grayling, for all its beauty and simple, wild willingness to take a fly, is a poor to average fighter. These Geike River grayling didn't fit the mold, if in fact there is such a mold. They ran, they jumped, they did cartwheels, and they struggled violently even as you held them in your hands and pulled the barb out. They were inordinately strong for their size.

And as I learned this day and was to relearn in days to come, these grayling, like so many of their brethren in habitats scattered across northern North America, preferred a dragging fly. When I switched to dry flies and let them swing downstream like dragging wet flies, the grayling would some-times follow the floating fly. But they wouldn't take it until it began to cut a wake in the water, as if the appearance of life-like movement against the current assured them that the in-sect they saw was not just a bit of dead flotsam. Or maybe, the fly was actually moving slower, in their perception, when it was dragging than when it was being carried along by the cur-rent, and thus it was easier to catch.

In his mammoth but incisive *Standard Fishing Encyclopedia*, Al McClane noted this tendency of the grayling to follow a fly and inspect it for some time, as if eager to accommodate the angler if everything appeared, finally, to be on the up-and-up. Grayling, he wrote, "have a common tendency to follow a fly before taking it; there's a bit of a time lag involved, and the upstream fly which floats back so quickly often moves but does not earn a fish." Another of the grayling's endearing traits is that when it does take a free-floating fly, it sometimes does so by making a spectacular, arching jump clear out of the water and then diving down on the fly from above—almost like a cat pouncing on a ball of yarn or a coyote on a mouse.

I don't know how many grayling the guide and I caught and released that day on the Geike, but the number was in the dozens. When we related our success back at camp, the Iowans decided it would be a nice lark to duplicate the experience the next day. When they returned from their voyage, I asked how they had done.

"We just caught three,"one guy complained. "Waste of time, mostly."

"What pattern did you use?"

"Pattern?"

"Yeah, what did you catch them on?"

"A Mepps spinner," he said.

I had forgotten these guys weren't fly-fishermen. But even that fact left me puzzled a bit, because grayling usually are willing to strike a small lure. Then I looked at their tackle and saw that they had affixed their spinners to the ten-inch wire leaders they had rigged earlier for pike fishing. Wilderness grayling may be naive, but they aren't blind.

On the rivers of Alaska, such as in the Bristol Bay region, grayling are never a "destination fish." Nobody goes there just to fish for grayling, although the quality of the grayling fishing in some areas is as good as light-tackle fly-fishing on the surface ever gets.

Alaska's Alagnak River, or Branch River, is home to a surprising variety of species, some of which are anadromous (salmon) and some of which (rainbow trout, grayling, Dolly Varden, and northern pike) aren't. It is possible at times on the Alagnak to fish at the same time and sometimes in the same run to king salmon, sockeye salmon, chum salmon, and big, resident rainbow trout. Therefore, thirteen- to eighteen-inch grayling, as beautiful and eager to please as they are, are back-shelved to a let's-take-a-break-and-fool-around-with-the-grayling status by most visitors. When your forearm, shoulder and wrist start to ache from casting 8-weight sink-tip lines and fighting ten- to thirty-pound fish, you stop for shore lunch at a grayling riffle, switch to a lighter rod, and play with the pretty little fish for awhile.

In a sense, though, grayling, with their delicate beauty and untamed, innocent exuberance, embody all that is best about wild and remote Alaska. When Lee Stearns and I elected to spend some three hours at one grayling run on the Alagnak, repeatedly hooking gorgeously colored fish both on dead-drifted dry flies and skittering or dragging dry flies (if they didn't take it on the dead drift, they took it on the drag), our guide looked at us a little strangely. He probably was wondering why a couple of dudes on a fairly expensive fishing vacation would rather spend time on grayling than on fresh-run salmon. Lee expressed it well enough. "You know," he said, as we motored back to the lodge for a hot shower and evening libations, "I suspect when I get back home, I'll wonder how I ever got enough of this fishing for grayling."

I have fished for grayling from Alaska to Canada to the Rocky Mountain West whenever the opportunity presented itself, and I have never been disappointed. But not all grayling are naive, sacrificial, and suicidal when presented with a fly or lure.

The most recent grayling I caught was a fourteen-incher from Pearl Lake in the Colorado mountains north of Steamboat Springs. They have been stocked there by the state fishery authorities, and some of them are now big enough to be state records. State-record-size grayling indeed are caught there from time to time, usually in the two or three weeks right after ice-out. But nobody gets to claim the fame, because the minimum size on a keeper fish of any species at Pearl (actually, the regulation was originally intended for trout) is eighteen inches. Any sixteen- to seventeen-inch grayling would likely be a state record, and several of those have been caught at Pearl, but somehow nobody has come up with an eighteen-inch-plus fish.

I fished for three hours before I caught that fourteen-inch grayling, which finally took a small Hare's Ear nymph fished on weighted leader. My wife and I were visiting the lake in July, long after the initial spring spate of dependable grayling action had abated. The limited number of grayling were now scattered and probably educated by being caught and released repeatedly in the ice-out period by local, in-the-know fishermen. Somehow, catching a grayling on this day, at this lake, became a significant challenge for me. My wife, visiting with a state park ranger back at the boat ramp, said the ranger pointed out across the bay to where I was wading and said, "Your husband certainly sticks with it, doesn't he?"

Grayling have a way of doing that to me.

CHAPTER 16

DAY OF THE SQUAWFISH

CHARLIE MEYERS AND I, AFTER BEING SHUTTLED BACK BY A friend from the spot downriver where we had parked our takeout vehicle, launched our canoe at the Highway 13 bridge over the Yampa River, south of Craig. The aluminum canoe would carry us, our rods, an assortment of lures and flies, a cooler of beer and sandwiches, and high hopes for an eight-mile venture into the joys of northern pike fishing.

"Not exactly the Canadian wilderness," Meyers said, shrugging at the passing traffic on the highway, "but pike are pike."

Actually, we would be in some fairly remote country a few miles downstream, but it would bear no resemblance to Canadian pike habitat. Setting out on a pike-fishing float on the Yampa in northwestern Colorado—or for that matter, any other river in the state—has a weird feel to it. The "water wolf" isn't supposed to be there and, in fact, had never been in the Yampa until about 1980, when pike suddenly started turning up on the flies, lures, or bait of stunned Yampa anglers expecting a trout or whitefish. ("Uh, Bubba, I don't know how to tell you this, but I think I caught a pike.")

Funny thing about many fish species—give them a chance to exist where they never have existed before and they'll do their damnedest to oblige. The fact that they often get the job done seems to say that, after all, the key ingredient in the survival of fish is the presence of water. And if the rest of the puzzle pieces fall into place—decent water quality, a reasonable range of water temperatures, sufficient forage and cover, adequate spawning habitat—you have yourself another species of fish, whether you want it or not.

Another characteristic that shouldn't be surprising to us is their ability to swim in or out of a body of still water if there's an inlet or an outlet. The pike in the Yampa—and some of them have reached the ten- to twenty-pound class—are there because their predecessors managed to migrate out of Elkhead Reservoir on Elkhead Creek, a tributary of the Yampa, and find their way down to the river. One of the messages here is that you need to be careful where you dump nonnative fish if you don't want them anywhere but the exact spot where you're dumping them.

There are some who view pike in the Yampa as a bonus angling opportunity on what is, in all honesty, a marginal trout stream. These are fishermen who delight in sampling a form of sport fishing that can be found only in a relatively limited number of places south of the Canadian border. There are others, such as trout purists and endangered-fish biologists, who view the escapement of pike into the Colorado River basin (of which the Yampa is a part) the same way they would a piranha turned loose in an exotic-fish aquarium, or a rather conspicuous turd afloat in the punch bowl. The Yampa, in addition to being the habitat of trout and mountain whitefish, is one of the last strongholds—or weakholds, if you prefer—of the Colorado squawfish, an officially endangered species. Trouble is, pike don't ask their potential dinner entree if it's in the salmonid family or a minnow on the endangered list, and they don't much give a damn either way. To that extent, they are a threat to both.

Meyers and I take the practical view that if you have a particular fish in a particular water, regardless of how it got there and whether or not it is indigenous to the water, you fish for it if it's a worthy adversary. Pike certainly qualify. Also, neither of us has the slightest aversion to a pile of pike fillets. We were more than willing to do our part to help save trout and squawfish.

That is not to say that either of us, as we slid the canoe into the murky currents of the Yampa and began to rediscover canoe-paddling skills that were rusty at best, had any particular affection for the squawfish. Neither of us had so much as held one in our hands. To us, they represented a rather expensive example of the national commitment to saving species teetering on the edge of disappearance. At times, some aspects of this mission (the boreal toad, the condor, and the whooping crane come to mind) seem to be a tedious and costly denial of the principle of survival of the fittest.

And both of us tend to reach for the grains of salt when we read or hear the pronouncements of federal or state endangered-species officials about how it will signal the collapse of the ecosystem if squawfish disappear from the upper Colorado River basin in Colorado, Wyoming, and Utah. Actually, the trout and the whitefish and the catfish and the suckers and the muskrats and the beavers and so forth will probably continue to do just fine.

To the extent that all of us should do what we can to save threatened species, I am sympathetic to the endangered-fish effort. But when we are told that some $137 million of public money will be spent on the Colorado River–basin recovery program before anybody even knows if it has a chance of being ultimately successful, I begin to wonder.

I continue to wonder when I hear that hydroelectric authorities on the Columbia River system are offering *bounties* for every dead Columbia River squawfish that sport fishermen can bring in. It seems that the squawfish up there eat steelhead and salmon smolts (they don't ask for IDs either before they chomp down on a victim), and the operators of the hydroelectric dams are bedeviled by all sorts of expenses and problems in trying to save threatened and endangered steelhead and salmon. This is as it should be—the mess is largely of their making. But the squawfish is just another thorn in their sides.

Surely, you are saying to yourself at this point, this clod knows there's a difference between a Columbia River squawfish and a Colorado squawfish. Of course there is, just as there's a difference (that is, a subspecies distinction) between a Tule elk and a Rocky Mountain elk, although I'd bet my worst graphite fly rod that the average citizen wouldn't know a Columbia River squawfish from a Colorado squawfish if you dumped both of them in his lap. As biologists point out, especially endangered-species biologists, a Louisiana black bear is not an Idaho black bear, a Florida cougar is not a Colorado cougar, a Snake River sockeye is not an Alaska sockeye, and an Atlantic sailfish is not a Pacific sailfish.

Still, it seems to me that the major difference in the case of the squawfish is that one lives in an area where it has dwindled perilously close to the precipice of extinction, and the other lives in an area where it is so abundant that it's a nuisance. One man's endangered species is another man's pain in the ass.

All of this was put out of mind as the two of us floated around a bend on the Yampa (after we spent an interesting interlude in fast, tricky water with us and the canoe floating backward) and enjoyed the sights and sounds of a big flock of Canada geese lifting into the air from a sandbar. On the sagebrush benches above the murky flow of the river, small herds of mule deer, garish ears cocked outward, foraged and paused to stare at our passing.

We soon beached the canoe at a likely looking run, got out to wade, and began casting. Something engulfed my Dardevle spoon on the third cast. The something came out of the water in a cartwheeling jump—a northern pike. It was a small one at about twenty inches, but it was a start. My next strike was telegraphed up through the light graphite spinning rod as a surprisingly solid wallop. Pike often simply stop a lure, as if it has run into a snag. This wasn't just a stop—it was an aggressive jolt, followed by some vigorous head shaking, and it reminded me of the initial impact of a striking white bass. This fish did no cartwheels. In fact, after the first ten seconds or so, there wasn't much fight at all. Pike sometimes relax until they are brought close to the angler and the net, so I was thinking pike again.

Then there was a last-second lunge and short run as the fish neared my wader-clad feet. It exhibited as much vigor at the last as it did on the strike. I was still thinking pike when I reached with the landing net and scooped up the eighteen-inch-long fish.

"What," asked Charlie, peering down into the net, "is *that*?"

"That," I said, barely able to believe it, "is a Colorado squawfish." I had seen enough photographs and artists' sketches of the species to know I was right. What it looked like was a toothless walleye with its face dished in. The contours and fins of the body resembled those of an overgrown fathead minnow on steroids.

"Well," Charlie said, "the endangered-fish boys are obviously right—there *are* some squawfish in the Yampa."

Two more squawfish were hooked and landed before we climbed back into the canoe to resume the float. The fish, of course, were duly released, although there was some tongue-in-cheek banter between us about wishing we had brought a frying pan. Who would know if a couple of canoeing klutzes dined on squawfish for shore lunch? (Of course, if they did somehow find out, we might be planning our next fishing trip from the cozy confines of a federal prison cell.)

We could pretend we were pioneer types subsisting on what the frontier citizens of western Colorado used to call "Colorado River salmon," or "white salmon." These fish were abundant in the Yampa, the White, the Green, the Colorado, the lower Gunnison, and other rivers. Colorado squawfish once reached weights more commonly associated with alligator gar or sturgeon—up to seventy-five pounds. Historical references tell us that early-day ranchers and farmers, right up through the Depression years, fished for and ate squawfish, sometimes catching huge specimens on ropelike setlines with such delicacies for bait as whole cottontail-rabbit heads.

Those stories—and there are old photos around to back them up—lend a sort of romantic slant to the struggle of the Colorado squawfish to sustain its place in history. Occasional specimens to thirty or thirty-five pounds are still discovered by researchers from time to time, but the fact is that the dams and water diversions on the Colorado River system have altered the flows, the water temperatures, and the water content so that squawfish are, in effect, trying to survive in a polluted remnant of their former habitat. Changes in salinity and temperature are bad enough, but the straw that appears to be breaking the backs of squawfish (and three other rough-fish endangered species in the system) is the presence of selenium. This natural element, contained in shale, is washed into the rivers in much greater volume than normal because of diversion water returned to the river from irrigated areas. It sterilizes the eggs of endangered species.

One federal study in a riverside pond found that not a single squawfish egg survived the efforts of spawning fish due to selenium contamination. Interestingly, this particular study was performed not by the U.S. Fish and Wildlife Service, which directs the recovery program while wielding the Endangered Species Act like a club, but by the U.S. Bureau of Reclamation. It is probably more than coincidental, in this instance, that the bureau has been forced to jump through all sorts of operational hoops to provide flow releases from dams that are more conducive to endangered-fish survival. (Why bother, they must wonder, if it won't make any difference?) If selenium is the real culprit, all the manipulated flows, research, endangered-fish stocking efforts, and the like—costing millions of dollars per year—may turn out to be useless.

The Yampa—from about Stagecoach Dam (upstream from Steamboat Springs) downstream through Craig, Maybell, and on to the river's juncture with the Green—contains a fascinating variety of fish species. It is possible to catch rainbow trout, brown trout, mountain whitefish, northern pike, smallmouth bass, and channel catfish—all in the same day if you work at it and don't mind traveling up or down the river. Some of the rainbows are of trophy size in the upper reaches, and the same can be said of the browns on the lower end.

But what we continued to catch on this strange float down the Yampa were Colorado squawfish. Once, we came to a level-depth, sweeping, side-channel run over clean gravel that seemed to be packed with them. A spoon or spinner allowed to sort of swim downstream and then swing across in the current was walloped with regularity by squawfish in the fourteen- to twenty-inch class. The bigger ones were remarkably colorful, with bright orange and red slashes along their flanks, as if they were in spawning colors. These no doubt were the males, but I am no squawfish expert.

Then again, maybe I am. Maybe Meyers and I both are, because all we caught, with the exception of one more pike, were squawfish, until our truck, parked in a rancher's haystack yard, came into view around a bend.

"Do you realize," I said to my partner as we beached the canoe, "that we have laid hands on more wild squawfish in one day than some of the fish biologists do in their careers?"

"These," he said, "are obviously very discriminating fish."

CHaPTer 17
Stranger in Steelhead country

THE SOFT OREGON RAIN ENVELOPED US WHEN WE STEPPED FROM the Portland air terminal. At times, rain in the Pacific Northwest doesn't so much fall as it seems to simply materialize—in the air, on the ground, all over everything.

"This will be gone in the morning," pronounced Leo Schmelz, frowning at the sky and struggling with rod cases and luggage.

It seemed important that my fishing partner, an eternal optimist whose meteorological musings were more often wrong than right, be right this time. We had flown 1,100 miles in early September from Colorado to seek summer steelhead, with visions of low, clear, blue-green rivers slicing through the lushness of coastal foliage. With the vision came the silver-streak shafts of leaping fish, erupting like missiles into late-summer sunlight. The vision never included rain, although in the back of my angler's mind was the sobering suspicion that fog and rain were more endemic to steelhead fishing than shirtsleeves and sun-block lotion.

We knew that the heavy, milky, rain-and-snow-swelled currents of winter produced heavier runs of fish and higher percentages of fishing success. But the truth was that we wanted, realistically or not, the rivers of Oregon to look, at least in clarity and size, somewhat like our Rocky Mountain trout streams. And we wanted to catch steelhead in essentially the same way we sometimes fished for trout back home—with light to ultra-light spinning rods and small, flashing lures. (The time was the mid-1970s, and we had not progressed yet in steelheading to the point where we felt comfortable fly-fishing for them.)

Spin-fishing often gets a bad rap from fly-fishermen because it is associated in some minds with treble-hook lures, bait-fishing, and unrestrained killing of fish, or simply because it gives the angler the advantage of being able to reach more water more quickly than with a fly rod. But there are special skills in adeptly using lures on light spinning tackle to probe the holding places of fish in moving water.

Further, fish can be released from the hook or hooks on a lure, just as they can be released from a fly. In my experience, the major problem with treble-hook lures is with small trout, fish in the eight- to twelve-inch range. In their gullibility, they somehow manage to get all three barbs inside their mouths. But barbs can be crimped down on lure hooks and trebles can be replaced with single hooks, no matter what the size of the fish. In fact, many savvy steelheaders remove the trebles from their favorite lures and replace them with Siwash-style, single hooks, because a single hook is easier to set and hold in the tough jaws of a big fish than a treble, and gives deeper penetration.

While hooking a steelhead or salmon on fly tackle is generally more difficult and requires more skill than doing it with spinning or bait-casting tackle, I am convinced that the advantage turns to the fly-fisherman once a big fish is hooked. There is less to go wrong on a good, drag-efficient, single-action fly reel, and the running, struggling fish must pull sixty-five or so feet of heavy fly line through the water. A hundred or two hundred feet of thin monofilament is not much of a hindrance, and whatever pressure is exerted in spin-fishing is accomplished totally by leverage of the rod. A lure can be thrown by the head-shaking gyrations of a fish. A fly cannot, although it may pull out or fall out. (In coming years, I would fish for steelhead exclusively with flies, but in my early days, the challenge of simply catching a steelhead made considerations about choice of method seem very academic.)

As for our collective expertise and knowledge about steelheading, Leo and I might as well have been equipped with Ouija boards and astrological charts. We were descending upon coastal Oregon with light tackle, high hopes, and a rental car to take us from river to river on the strength of not a lot more than optimistic whim. This expedition had all the predictability of a gypsy migration.

For once, Leo's optimism was vindicated. Brilliant, late-morning sunshine cascaded from a sky that was blue from horizon to horizon. The passing of the rain was recorded only in remnant stains on the highway. We drove with nervous eagerness up Oregon Highway 224, past the town of Estacada along the canyon of the Clackamas River.

The Clackamas—a tributary of the brooding Willamette and a summer-run river that in the 1970s and 80s gave up to anglers maybe 2,500 summer steelhead in a season. The Clackamas is a compromise between the desertlike environs of Oregon's eastern-slope rivers such as the Deschutes and the lush richness of the state's coastal-forest streams. Along the Clackamas, the forest is there, thick and gloomy, but the river is swift and rock-ribbed, like an Idaho or Montana river. Our choice of the Clackamas for the first day was grounded in tackle-shop chatter from earlier in the morning, when we had purchased licenses, and in dimly remembered magazine stories about steelhead fishing.

The choice seemed a good one. The river was low and clear and would pose a good test for our light-tackle theories, which held that you did not need a long, heavy drift rod, ten-pound-test line, and a sack of roe with pencil-lead sinker to catch steelhead—at least not in summer-clear water. With our darting, swimming spinner lures and four-pound line (six-pound at most), we would appeal not to half-forgotten feeding habits, but to instinctive, lightning-quick aggressiveness.

As I drove, Leo pointed up the canyon. "Look—a reservoir. Can the fish get past it?"

"Yeah. See the fish ladder?" A series of rundown-looking locks and chutes stair-stepped uphill, around the dam.

"I hope they use it," Leo said, dubiously.

We parked the rented station wagon in a U.S. Forest Service picnic ground. I suggested that my friend try the pocket water just upstream while I heated lunchtime soup for us on our one-burner stove. "You sure they're here?" Leo muttered again before heading off to push through the riverside alders.

The chicken noodle had barely begun to boil when I heard the familiar whoop that meant my partner had hooked a good fish. I trotted in his direction and emerged from the alders in time to see the last, twisting leap of a brilliant silver steelhead, maybe ten pounds. The fish crashed back with a loud slap. The blade of the little spinner winked in the sunlight as it, too, fell free to the river. Leo's rod straightened, his shoulders slumped, and he reeled in his trailing line.

"I think they're here," I said. "Soup's on."

After lunch, we fished hard. The river gave off a keen, intense edge of adventure, the feeling that only big fish in modest-size water can generate. Walking up to a steelhead river instills a state of mind totally unlike the pleasant, casual expectation that surrounds many other forms of fishing. A steelhead river gives off suspense and intenseness, like a vapor. The atmosphere is energized by the knowledge that these runs and pockets and pools and riffles, which may superficially reveal only the surface dimples of feeding smolts, conceal fish that can literally smash your tackle if you aren't paying close attention. Steelhead bring drama to a river. Everything that happens, or doesn't happen, takes on transcendental dimensions. Of course, you are never sure just what *will* happen, if indeed anything does, but you are pretty damned sure that whatever does happen will happen fast, and sometimes with no warning whatsoever. Mostly, the feeling is one of awe, that eight- to fifteen-pound, anadromous trout could be in a river of this size, and that some occult sensitivity has brought them from the ocean, past a dozen or more other rivers, to find this particular one—the river of their beginnings.

We worked steadily upstream, using six-foot rods and (in Leo's case) four-pound- and (in my case) six-pound-test line. Despite the promise engendered by Leo's earlier hookup, we were rewarded only by steelhead and salmon smolts, eight to twelve inches—the size of fish colloquially referred to in Oregon as "trout."

Our total steelheading experience until now had amounted to only a couple of days on Oregon coastal streams a few years earlier, on a trip that was more productive for offshore salmon. Leo and I had failed to land a single steelhead in that week, although the magic and mystery of steelhead had touched us in the form of strikes and lost fish, and a partner had actually managed to catch one. We had learned that a strike from a big steelhead could be as subtle as the take of a ten-inch trout.

As early afternoon wore into evening without another hookup for either of us, weariness and futility began to set in like the first funkiness of a flu virus. Casts became mechanical; retrieves were hurried or laxly attended to. This quest for steelhead had the makings, as any obsession does, of fruitless frustration and bitter disappointment. Sometimes, it seems that success on big fish is inversely proportional to how deeply you covet the fish. The more burning the obsession and the longer the siege of futility, the more elusive the goal. Atlantic salmon fishermen and pursuers of permit on the flats know this feeling intimately.

Leo, wading and casting restlessly, moved out of sight upstream. I came upon a long, deep hole with gliding current over deeply submerged boulders at its tail. I knew that pocket tailwater with sufficient depth was attractive to resting steelhead. I stared through my Polaroids into the green water. My enthusiasm was renewed at the sight of a fish flashing in the depths. It had turned, catching the slanting sunlight. Then, I saw more flashes—too many to be steelhead, and too small. I realized finally that I was probably seeing a cluster of whitefish. But I cast anyway, halfheartedly, toward a barrel-size boulder two feet under the surface. A narrow band of shadow lined the underside of the boulder.

I was using a fluorescent-red-bodied, silver-bladed No. 3 Rooster Tail, figuring the color would trigger spawning anger. On the third cast, the lure flashed past the shadow under the rock, and a part of the shadow separated itself from the rock and moved for the lure. The steelhead was big and incomprehensibly quick. But it missed the single hook I had rigged on the lure or perhaps turned away from it at the last instant. The shadow sank back to its rock.

I kept casting. I had seen a steelhead and I was reluctant to leave it. Then something out of my trout-fishing experience came to me—a change of lure color sometimes induces a strike from a fish that has already moved to a lure. I removed the red lure and replaced it with a black-bodied Rooster Tail. The lure sailed out, settled into the water upstream of the rock and began to swing against the current, through the rock's shadow and back toward the light. It never made it. It stopped as if fouled on the rock. I set the hook as hard as I could with the light rod. The steelhead came up immediately, a good two feet over the surface, fell back, then was off on an upstream run. I set the hook again to be sure. The steelhead was in the air again, arcing recklessly, falling back stiff-sided with a smack. Its speed and strength were stunning—difficult to fathom. The reel's drag whined. On the third jump, the fish and the lure parted. I was beginning to understand that light rods were not all that great as a tool for steelhead hook-setting. For a moment, I neither moved nor breathed. A curse came on the breath that finally escaped. I waded out of the river, sat down on the rocks, and stared between my wader-clad legs, at nothing, for what seemed a long time.

We needed a new river—new hope. We had a couple pieces of information to work with, one old and one new. The old was what had come of a meeting, on our previous Oregon trip, with a coastal resident who had previously lived in Denver. We had been advised to look him up and seek counsel on fishing. We had met him in a dim bar, where the lighting gave sinister contrast to his darkly bearded face. He struck me as looking like Rasputin, though I had only a vague notion of what Rasputin looked like. Rasputin had swallowed some of his beer and laughed, "Four-pound line? Light rods? You guys are crazy. But I think I love it."

Rasputin had recommended the Nestucca River, a relatively unpublicized coastal river near Tillamook, a primarily winter-run river that is overshadowed by waters such as the

Rogue and the Umpqua, farther to the south. His information had been good. It was on the Nestucca, on that trip, that we had enjoyed what little success we had previously recorded in our quixotic joustings with the gods of steelheading.

The current information came from an Oregon state-highway patrolman who had checked our fishing licenses. "I hear they're doing pretty good on steelhead over on the Trask," he said, referring to another river near Tillamook. Oregon is the only state I have fished where state troopers make fishing-license checks. It is an interesting concept in shared duty. I wondered if Oregon game wardens wrote speeding tickets.

The Trask, as near as we could tell, held few if any steelhead, despite the patrolman's information. Unusually low and clear, what it did hold was a phalanx of chinook salmon, far upstream on their spawning run, ranging in deterioration from red through stained copper to almost black. They struck a lure—or nipped at it—with surprising regularity.

I landed and released a twenty-three-pound female that had been holding in a narrow slot at the head end of a run. The fight was disappointing, not because the fish lacked strength or bulk, but because for most of the struggle it refused to move at all. This hen was too close in calendar terms to her destiny, and she had limited reserves for warding off forces that interfered with her reproductive mission.

Leo hooked a red-sided male that was faster, stronger, more active, and more determined. Probably thirty-five pounds, the hook-jawed fish led him on an awkward, rock-hopping chase down through a fast narrows on the half-dry riverbed. I stumbled along dutifully behind, lugging my Nikon and Leo's home movie camera.

His slender glass rod strained dangerously, affording no real leverage on such a fish. When I finally caught up with him, he was disgustedly tossing what was left of the rod up onto the bank. It had shattered just above the ferrule. It was only the second time I had ever seen a rod broken strictly by the strength of a fish. Most stories like this are wishful thinking.

One day of this undergunning on salmon was enough. While school was still out on our use of light spinning gear for steelhead, it was obvious that big salmon were a bit too much. Dark, about-to-spawn chinook, or king salmon, while they provided a certain bullish thrill on peashooter tackle, were not bright, fresh-run fish, and it didn't seem right to stress them this late in their cycle—and certainly not with tackle so slight that it required too long to bring the fish to hand.

And the fact remained that they were not steelhead. We left the Trask and took a motel in Tillamook, talking of the prospects for tomorrow—and the Nestucca.

We lingered over second cups of coffee in the motel coffee shop, surrounded by log-truck drivers and others bent on gloomy, predawn assignments. We peered out sweating windows at a blend of fog and misting rain. Leo's bluebird interlude had played out the string. He looked as glum as the weather. But to me, the rain looked soft and friendly. I felt confident, almost relaxed.

"A steelhead morning," I heard myself saying. "If ever there was one, this is it. Not enough rain to murk up the river, but the flat light will keep the fish moving longer. The hell with sunshine. It hasn't done us much good so far." My friend did not argue, but he looked discouraged. We finished our greasy, overfried eggs, paid the check, and walked out into the rain.

Dawn came in small, gray increments as we drove toward the crossroads hamlet of Beaver, where we turned east to follow the course of the Nestucca. It is, or was at that time, one of Oregon's finer steelhead streams, then producing several thousand fish per year—a small percentage being summer-run fish. We parked near a highway bridge and prepared our tackle. The verdant lushness of dairy farms and meadows was accentuated by the caressing fog and drizzle. A young girl was herding two heavy-uddered cows to the barn for milking. Blackberries blossomed in lush bounty along a fence beside the highway, their ripeness made more apparent by a sheen from the clinging raindrops.

Again, I was surprised by the relative lack of fishing pressure on summer steelhead on some Oregon rivers. We had seen few fishermen on the Trask and Clackamas. There were none here. Perhaps the locals didn't get serious about their steelheading until the rivers swelled with winter torrents, when larger thrusts of fish migrated across river-mouth estuaries. The novelty of our maverick approach was wearing thin for lack of holes in our steelhead punch cards.

There was an elbow-shaped run behind a neat farm upstream from the bridge. We hopscotched our way upstream, casting intently, expectancy hanging on every retrieve. The mist shrouded the river, transforming its green color to an almost opaque gray.

I kept casting with stubborn, mechanical persistence. I wanted, more than anything I could recall wanting in fishing, to be able to say that I had "killed" a steelhead on light trout tackle on a rainy, foggy morning in Oregon. I would use the word with the same proud bluntness of those who spoke not of catching but of "killing" an Atlantic salmon. I had never fished for Atlantic salmon and I probably never would, but I was beginning to suspect that there was little they could show me in terms of a challenge that I had not already embraced here on the summer steelhead waters of the Pacific Northwest.

I moved past Leo and walked up to the very head of a reach of fast water, where the run was born in a wide, swift, shallow riffle over cobblestone rocks. The gray light made it impossible to discern shapes below the surface, but I kept reminding myself that a ten-pound fish could be invisible in ten inches of water under these conditions.

I cast to the shallowest upper portion of the riffle and cranked in slack line as I let the lure drift down, its undulating silver blade and black bucktail carried along by the current into an almost imperceptibly deeper slot. The lure stopped with a light tapping sensation. I guessed that I had hooked another smolt, or perhaps a small cutthroat trout.

I set the hook anyway, with force.

Steelhead!

It raged upstream toward the narrow neck of the riffle in the shallow water, throwing spray with its tail. It must have thought better of this, because it turned and bolted downstream, then stood on its head in a crazy jump that left my rod and line sickeningly slack for an instant. But the steelhead was still there, sending violent protests up through the rod. The fish was swimming downstream, toward the distant highway bridge. I stumbled after it, slipping on the rain-slick rocks. The steelhead reached the deeper water of the lower run, where it settled down to a head-into-the-current fight that began to betray its stamina. For the first time in this light-tackle lark through Oregon, I felt in control of a steelhead.

The rest was anticlimactic, although there was one sickening moment just before I beached the fish when I thought it had fallen free of the lure. It had not. This was a hen steelhead, about nine pounds. Leo's congratulations were somewhat subdued, tempered with the reality that he had not landed a steelhead of his own.

"Try that same riffle," I said. "Sometimes these fish move in pairs."

My companion shrugged, picked up his rod, and walked back toward the head of the run. He was one of the finer lure fishermen I had ever met, and if there was one more willing steelhead there to entice, he would do it.

It happened on his second cast. Not more than six feet from where my fish had hit, another one accepted his lure. The fish burst off on a dazzling run. I yelled for Leo to set the hook again. I don't know if he heard me, but the rod came up, perhaps reflexively. The fight settled down to a nerve-jangling game of varying degrees of rod and drag pressure, with the steelhead husbanding its strength, expending energy reluctantly. At last the buck steelhead, almost the same size and length as mine, was flopping on the gravel. It was a glistening, nickel-bright presence—the brightest thing in a dim, misty morning. Steelhead morning, I thought again, seeing the wide grin on my partner's wet face. I repeated it aloud: "Steelhead morning."

He nodded happily. I reached into a pocket for a celebratory cigar. The fog had begun to creep away from the cradle of the river, stealing back into the alders and firs like a thief caught in the act. Or more, I thought, like a fleeting fisherman's blessing withdrawn to be bestowed on another day, on another river. No longer were we strangers in steelhead country.

I returned periodically to the steelhead rivers of Oregon and Washington over a period of several years, not completely realizing at the time that I was sampling something that was dwindling away inexorably, like sand through an hourglass. These pilgrimages took me to, among other rivers, the Clackamas, the Nestucca, the Wilson, the Trask, and the Deschutes in Oregon, and in Washington, the Lewis, the Kalama, and the Toutle, before a volatile event named St. Helens turned it into a gush of hot mud and debris.

The 1970s and early 1980s constituted a sort of modern peak in Pacific Northwest steelhead fishing. The steelhead and salmon runs on the Columbia and Snake rivers—particulary the Idaho steelhead, chinook salmon, and sockeye salmon—were beginning to succumb to the gauntlet of dams and slow-pool backwaters that blocked their upstream migrations as adults and confused their downstream journeys as smolts. In 1986, some 3.2 million salmon and steelhead entered the Columbia on spawning runs; in 1994, the estimate was 856,500 fish.

Today, there are good runs of mostly hatchery steelhead on some Columbia tributaries. Some steelhead still make it back to their home rivers in Idaho. There have been good summer runs in recent years on the Deschutes in Oregon, in part, ironically, because some of the fish that should return to other parts of the Columbia system "get lost" as strays in the slack water and settle for the Deschutes.

More than 80 percent of the steelhead harvested in Oregon, Washington, and Idaho are hatchery fish—detectable, usually, by their clipped adipose fins. Wild fish are outnumbered on most of the coastal rivers by an average of at least two to one—in some instances by four to one. Some wild steelhead strains are listed as endangered. The sockeye salmon of the Snake River are endangered—extinct, in practical terms. The

Snake River chinook salmon are officially "threatened." Environmental groups and some federal officials believe it is time to "list" other salmon species along the coast. But salmon are a sad story for another book.

State and federal officials in Washington, Oregon, and California continue to haggle over which populations of wild steelhead should or shouldn't be listed as threatened or endangered. Meanwhile, in many cases, the very existence of hatchery fish, however worthy they may be on the end of a line, threatens the genetic integrity of wild strains. Offspring of hatchery steelhead, or of the mating of hatchery fish with wild fish, generally don't survive.

Steelhead fishing could close entirely on some productive rivers if their wild populations are accorded threatened or endangered status. At this time, the feds are pushing to list steelhead stocks on certain southern Oregon rivers, such as the Chetco, as threatened. The irony of the Chetco is that its wild steelhead are in better shape than most, partly because its headwaters are in a protected wilderness area, where logging and development are prevented.

Steelhead were doing fine until the 1960s, when the inexorable tide of human machinations began to take its toll. Development, clear-cutting, overgrazing, other habitat problems that destroyed spawning areas, dewatering and diversion, the runaway construction of dams, changes in the ocean currents and fertility (which hurt survival of young fish), commercial fishing, sport-fishing pressure, and finally, dependency on hatchery runs, all have played a part. Court decisions that clarified Indian commercial and subsistence fishing rights are blamed by some observers, but that element probably has been overemphasized.

"When the hatchery programs got rolling, the word got out about the bigger runs and the sport-fishing pressure increased," said Bob Hooton of the Oregon Fish and Wildlife Department. "The dams and the development and all the rest, along with overfishing and the effect hatchery fish had on wild genetics—it all began to add up. Things started to fall apart in the mid-1980s."

Bruce Sanford, steelhead manager for the Washington Fish and Wildlife Department, is realistic about the steelhead picture. "I try to be optimistic," he said, "but I don't think things are going to get a lot better. We don't have any control, for instance, over the land-management practices that go on out here. We just have to try to retain what we've got."

Most of my experience with steelhead has been with summer fish. In the early 1980s, I revisited the Clackamas in the company of Jim Teeny of Gresham, Oregon, who taught me an effective way to take summer steelhead on fly tackle. I had long entertained notions of nymph fishing for steelhead, just as I nymph fished for trout in my Rocky Mountain streams, but my mental picture of doing this entailed standard nymph patterns such as stonefly nymphs—even though I knew that steelhead do little spawn-run feeding in fresh water.

Jim Teeny took this concept a step further and made it work. He took a scruffy-looking "nymph" that he invented for fishing a west-slope Oregon trout lake—a concoction he originally dubbed the "Abduli"—and parlayed it into a line of varicolored and multisized flies now marketed under the name "Teeny Nymph." In truth, Jim's pattern, constructed out of pheasant-tail fibers—sometimes dyed, sometimes not—was more a wet fly or a shrimp imitation than a nymph. But he dead-drifted it for steelhead as if it were a nymph, in natural color, dyed black, dyed green, ginger, pink, red, and you-name-it. He even patented the pattern, which didn't stop anybody from copying it, but it presumably did stop them from marketing it under the same name.

There are fly-fishing steelheaders who view dead-drift, weighted-pattern, or weighted-leader nymphing tactics as a vulgar, demeaning way to pursue this magnificent game fish. Many of them catch steelhead with traditional wet-fly or streamer patterns and mend-and-swing tactics, or not at all. Some take it a step further and fish for steelhead almost exclusively with surface flies. (The late Roderick Haig-Brown, the dean of western fly-fishing writers, believed that summer steelhead were easier to take on surface flies than any other way.)

I have no problem with these pure approaches and can admire the rationale behind them. What I can't appreciate or admire is the sort of deprecatory judgment that says another angler's method, however legal and demanding of skill, is to be sneered at. Or maybe it's just that in my case, merely *catching* steelhead is so much of a challenge that splitting hairs over fly-fishing approaches to get the job done seems ridiculously esoteric—like debating whether the chicken or the egg arrived on the scene first. The fact is, the chickens are here, and does it really matter?

Jim Teeny's larger contribution to steelhead and salmon fishing has been the development of a line of specialty fly lines, full sinkers, slow sinkers, and sink tips that cover a range of fishing needs according to type of water and fishing approach.

When Teeny, Joe Butler, and I fished one July for a surprisingly thick run of summer steelhead (mostly hatchery fish) on the Clackamas, we hooked maybe two dozen steelhead in three days. I say "we," but they did most of the hooking and certainly the lion's share of the landing. In the low, clear water, the fish were holding in the fast water at the heads of runs, where the water was more oxygenated and the choppy surface gave steelhead a sense of security.

I found ways to lose steelhead that went beyond even my previously extensive inventory of screw-ups. Somehow, on that trip, it all seemed foreordained for me, as if I were laboring under a curse that had to run its course.

Yet there were other trips when things went right—again on the Nestucca, where one dusky evening, two ten-pounders were beached inside a half-hour, and on a brilliantly sun-dazzled day on the Deschutes, an eight-pounder was brought to net just before I slipped off a lava ledge and bobbed in the river like a cork. (Both I and the steelhead reached the bank—both of us very wet.)

Still, the defeats, if they can be called that, burn as bright in the memory as the triumphs—which, after all, may be what sets steelheading apart from other forms of fishing. There was the estimated fifteen-pound, summer-run buck steelhead, a giant for where he was and the time of year I hooked him, that fought like a deep-slugging salmon on a long run called the Chicken Inn Drift on the Kalama, as my guide maneuvered the drift boat while trying to coach me on how to reattach the handle to the fly reel. The handle had simply fallen off the reel spool during the fight, and after failing to screw it back into the spool, I resorted to hand retrieving and releasing line as the fight demanded. Little by little, palming the spool, I managed to get the line back on the handleless reel. That fish was whipped, or so I thought, when it rolled at boatside. Now, I said to myself, is the time to use the eight-and-one-half-foot rod and six-pound leader to the full extent of their strength. I clamped my palm down harder on the rim of the reel spool at exactly the same instant the steelhead recovered and lunged downward toward the bottom of the river. The leader parted with a loud pop, like a muffled shot from a small-bore rifle.

At the time, nothing mattered more than the fact that I had blown it. Now, nothing matters more than the fact that the steelhead was there, and for a time, I was there with it.

CHAPTER 18

THE GREAT LAND

THE PILOT BANKED OUR PLANE AND CROSSED HIGH OVER THE WIDE ribbon of water gliding through the green tundra. I looked down toward the surface of the river from my seat against a window and saw what looked to be wavy lines of smoke, or stains like gray ink, trailing in the clear water with a wavering pattern close to the north bank of the river. The lines followed the contours of the river channel and the beckoning pull of the current.

The lines were not smoke, nor were they ink. They were disciplined processions of spawn-run salmon, sockeyes, and chums, forging upstream in their pursuit of nature's plan—its guarantee of regeneration, and inevitably, of death. It was July, and three species of salmon—including a vanguard of the majestic kings—were on their spawning runs up Southwest Alaska's Alagnak River in the Bristol Bay region.

As our plane throttled down, pointing for the newly carved dirt strip at Tony Sarp's Katmai Lodge on a breezy bluff, we could see below us the blue metallic bulk of a float plane resting atop the spongy green carpet of the tundra. Looking mostly intact, the high-and-dry plane was no more than thirty yards from the edge of the river. The fuselage, gleaming in the late-morning light, was resting upright on damaged pontoons. It looked for all the world as if some giant, mischievous hand had plucked if off the river and dropped it there. The main damage seemed to be to the pontoons.

Spotting the stranded plane, one of our group, arriving for a week's fishing, asked the pilot how it happened to get there. As he made a second swing, checking the wind for his final approach, the pilot explained: "A young fisherman from Italy was one of the passengers in that plane. He was sitting in the copilot's seat. Just as the plane was lifting off the river, he panicked and grabbed the controls. Luckily, nobody was injured." If the guy sitting next to our pilot felt any nervous compunction to assist the pilot in landing the plane, he stifled it.

A few days later, setting the hook into another muscular chum salmon that ran off my fly line into the backing, I thought of the cracked-up plane and began to have sympathy for the Italian angler with the grabby hands. Hell, after a week of fishing in Alaska, maybe his nerves were shot.

Strangely, though, the physical act of fighting an Alaska salmon—king (chinook), silver (coho), chum (dog), sockeye (red), or, in alternate years, pink (humpy) salmon—is a calming experience compared to the contemplation of the encounter itself. To an Alaska newcomer, awe and nervousness surround the event, bracketing it before and after each fish is hooked. But once the fish is solidly hooked and the first panic-choked minutes are out of the way, the fighting of the fish seems more calming and familiar (although the size of it certainly may not be familiar) than simply realizing in advance that it is there, along with all the others that inhabit the rivers of Alaska.

When a first-time Alaska angler wades out and faces not several, not dozens, but perhaps hundreds of passing fish from five to fifty pounds (depending on the species), there is always a moment when he wonders if any of it is real—and whether he has the skills, the stamina, and the tackle to do battle with these sea-fattened creatures. The magnitude of the resource is staggering.

And those are just the anadromous fish. The big, resident rainbows with wide, crimson stripes looking as if some zany artist with a Van Gogh complex swiped a paintbrush down their sides are present all the time on rivers such as the Alagnak, hiding along the brush-lined side channels and hovering below main-current drop-offs. Sometimes they are hard to find when the salmon pass through, as if they want no part of this crude traffic congestion; other times they hang right in with the salmon spawners and prey on the eggs.

There are rivers in Alaska, and the Alagnak is just one where a fly-fisherman can hook so many grayling, barely moving his feet, that he becomes jaded. Depending on the river, there are also northern pike, Dolly Varden, whitefish, sheefish, and, in some areas, steelhead, char, and lake trout. But there are relatively few river camps where, at the right time of the summer, you can catch seven different species—as you can at Katmai Lodge—without flying out at least once to a different area.

There are different ways to fish Alaska, and the way we were doing it—flying in to a first-class camp with all (or most of) the amenities—has a dangerous tendency to mislead you. Because you have been whisked there with the speedy and relatively painless technology of jet airliners and float planes, delivered almost to the door of your heated cabin, you may forget that you are, after all, in a wilderness. You may travel up or down the river in a jet boat, your guide may serve you a gourmet shore lunch, and you may have your container of vodka Gibson mix and your cooler full of lager beer along to comfort you. But if something happened to the guide or the boat, you'd still be umpteen miles back in a bear-inhabited wilderness with no way to walk back. Then, it would be up to you and the tenacity of your guts.

My partner on this trip, Lee Stearns, floated this same river a few years earlier, without a guide, in a rubber raft. He was dropped off in the headwaters by a float pilot who picked him and his companion up a week later on the lower end. He caught relatively few fish because he spent a lot of his time just trying to make sure he got safely to the other end. As he related, there are no illusions about your status under those conditions, or about where you are. He walked around with a .357 Magnum handgun on his hip and laughed about it later when knowledgeable friends suggested that an Alaska grizzly, right after he shot it with a puny .357, would place the pistol up his ass for safekeeping.

I write of the Alagnak by name with some misgivings. There are more and more boats on the river, and the permanent camps, few though they are, seem to get bigger each year. There is a temptation to think of Alaska's fish resources the same way many people used to think of the oceans—that they cannot be depleted. But we know better now. Humans have the capacity to deplete or destroy any resource, and those who value Alaska must never take it for granted.

Alaska is often called the Last Frontier of North American fishing. When Secretary of State William Seward pushed for the purchase of Alaska from Russia in 1867, for what some called the outrageously inflated price of $7.2 million, scoffers wondered what this godforsaken terrain could possibly hold besides Eskimos, bears, and icicles. They called it Seward's icebox. But to most who go to, live in, or dream of Alaska, including anyone who gets his kicks on the business end of a fly rod, it is, simply, the Great Land.

Declan Hogan, our guide, squinted into the afternoon light, flattened now by the scudding gray clouds, and apparently saw what he was looking for on the pewter surface sheen of the river. He turned the jet boat in a sharp bend to the left, throttled down, and deftly slid the big, sledlike boat onto a gravel bar.

Lee Stearns and I, already wearing waders, climbed over the gunwales of the boat, reaching for fly rods. I looked at the riffle just downstream from the boat. The surface of the river appeared to have come to life, rippling and wriggling like the skin of some awakening animal shaking off a chill. The vibrant life below the surface was bulging and moving, creating wakes, and even to an angler who was not an Alaska veteran, it was apparent that this was a staggeringly thick school of big sockeye salmon, forging upstream and fresh from saltwater.

"This must be the place," Stearns said, grinning.

I had rigged a big Hardy fly reel with floating fly line on a 7-weight graphite rod. The leader was nine feet, tapered to six-pound test. I twisted on a strip of matchbook lead above a No. 10 pink streamer I had tied at home in Colorado. "Sockeyes love pink," a friend had told me back in Denver when I had planned my first Alaska trip. (Actually, they can exhibit a strong interest at any given time in blue, red, chartreuse, orange, silver, or other colors as long as they are flashy and presented in a mostly dead-drift, passive way. At other times, perversely, they can be the most aloof of fish.)

This was my second shot at Alaska fishing. Two years earlier, I had spent a week in the area, dividing the time between the Alagnak and Brooks rivers. It had been one of the strangest, most nontypical weeks of weather ever experienced by Tony Sarp, owner of Katmai Lodge, his staffers, and his repeat guests.

It rained lightly for precisely two hours the day of my arrival on that first trip, and then the sun shone and shone and shone. By midweek, Ed Rice and I were fishing in shirtsleeves, slathering on sunscreen, and cooking in the merciless glare of a sun that seemed to be lowering itself through air that was more like an oppressive, breathless vacuum. The temperature was eighty-five degrees. We had somehow found ourselves in skin-cancer country, victims of the most unimaginable kind of meteorological aberration. Most of the clothing we had packed was too heavy. To the southeast, the iron-gray haze of drifting smoke appeared, the residue of brush, grass, and forest fires. The base of the Alaska Peninsula was baking in a drought.

"Incredible," our guide said, maneuvering us to and from schools of chums and sockeyes that actually darted away from fly lines and leaders. The river was painfully low and clear, and the relentless sun penetrated all the way to bottom in even the deeper channels.

"I've never seen Alaska salmon this spooky," said Rice. ("Spooky," of course, is a relative term in this instance. Instead of getting a strike, say, every three casts, you get one every fifteen casts.)

Once, as we were drifting with the drought-diminished current in a kind of collective stupor along a side channel, mechanically casting deer-hair mice to grassy edges and occasionally hooking somewhat small, lethargic rainbows, I decided to pull off a little joke. I was lying back in the boat, taking a break, and slurping at a rapidly warming beer. Rice was in the bow, casting. Thinking of the beer, I looked up intently into the dazzling orb of the sun and shouted, "No, God," and added in a lower voice, "I said a *Bud Light!*" (Reference, of course, to the old television commercials.)

Rice, who had heard clearly only the first two words and misinterpreted them, dropped his rod, turned to me in a panic, and said, "Oh, Lord, Bob, what?"

Later, he explained, "I thought you were crying 'Oh God.' Hell, I thought you were having a heart attack—or at least a sunstroke."

Now, on my second Alaska pilgrimage, as I prepared to cast to this massive school of moving sockeyes, it was obvious that there would be no sunburn, low-water curse on this second trip. The air was cold enough for a down parka, clouds were gathering that would bring light rain every day of our stay, the river was high but clear, and conditions couldn't be better for taking fresh-run sockeyes. In other words, Alaska weather.

I made my first cast, mended line, and watched the tip of the floating fly line for any sign of a hesitation. I had learned the first year that sockeyes, even when in a taking mood, do not often hammer a fly or lure—they simply mouth it and nip at it, as if curious. If the fly line jumps and the fish bolts maniacally in any direction long enough to strip the fly line backing off the reel, the fish is probably foul-hooked.

The light green line slowed and then stopped. I came up on the eight-and-a-half-foot rod and felt the immediate surge of the fish. It bolted, but not far, and then it came out in one of those crazy, cartwheeling jumps that left it standing on its head, momentarily married to the surface film in a kind of French kiss for what seemed like a significant slice of eternity. Then it crashed back. It was definitely fair-hooked, and this first salmon—first fish, in fact—of my second visit to Alaska was the biggest sockeye I had ever seen.

The gist of any successful fight with a strong fish is knowing when to give and when to take, and I recollected the indirect advice I had gotten from Ed Rice—promoter of sportsmen's expositions and one of this country's finer fly casters and anglers—a few years earlier: "After I hook a big fish," he said, "either the fish is taking line or I am taking line. I don't let the fish rest." For awhile with this red salmon, I wondered if it was simply not letting *me* rest. But finally, the huge sockeye, so deep through the girth that it seemed inflated like a football, was in the shallow water with its backside protruding, and I slid it with my hands up onto the gravel.

Dec Hogan was impressed—not by me so much as by the fish. "That sockeye is well over eleven pounds," he said. I learned later that it might well have been a tippet-class, fly-rod world record, but we never weighed or recorded it officially. What we did was eat it back at the lodge. The only reason I felt guilty about it was the fact that it wasn't even the main course. Broiled salmon fillets do a nice job, though, of complementing prime rib roast.

Somehow, chum salmon, or "dog" salmon as they are called by Alaskans, have gotten a bad rap. (The reference, depending on which version you believe, has to do with natives feeding their sled dogs with the flesh of chum salmon, or with the fact that the dark males with their garish kypes and sharp teeth look like snarling dogs.) Chum salmon or dog salmon—whatever you call them—are to me two different fish with two different personalities, but both add up to bulldog-tough, don't-give-an-inch fighters. They are possibly the strongest salmon in the world for their size. (Not the most spectacular or acrobatic, just pound-for-pound the strongest, although perhaps not possessing as much stamina as other salmon species.)

The first personality is the one you see when you intercept a chum salmon that is still fairly bright and fresh from the sea. This is a fast and surprisingly acrobatic fish, at times leaping like an overgrown sockeye or a silver salmon. The second, which has been the source of some disparagement by anglers, is one that has been in the fresh water of its home river for awhile. It is darkly colored—some might say in an ugly way— and the males have pronounced kypes and sharp teeth. (I once performed first aid on an Alaska guide whose thumb had been sliced open in the jaws of a chum salmon. I poured vodka out of a flask to try to sterilize the wound; it apparently worked, because the cut never got infected.)

It doesn't take long for the spawning metamorphosis to make itself plain in a chum salmon: One day the salmon is bright green and clean on its sides, and in the next day or two it looks like some graffiti artist swiped jagged olive or maroon stains down the fish's flanks—or that somebody spilled paint on the dorsal surface and it dripped down in outrageous, irregular patterns. When hooked, these darker fish jump less frequently and sometimes not at all.

If you want to get acquainted with the best of the two personalities, head in the direction of tidewater. Somewhere close to it, if you are there the right week, you will find the fresh chum salmon, averaging ten to fifteen pounds, moving upriver. We found them, and we fished for them with eight-weight rods and sink-tip lines, casting across current and mending as best we could until the streamer fly—an Egg-Sucking Leech worked well, along with anything pink or fiery orange—was sinking and swimming and then beginning to swing. Then we waited for the jolt. The strike was not the usually subtle strike of, for instance, a silver or sockeye salmon.

And when the jolt comes, all hell breaks loose. Strong, skilled fly-fishermen such as Ed Rice and Dec Hogan do a masterful, clever job of landing fresh chum salmon very fast, leveraging the rod this way and that, often holding the rod low to the water, and putting their shoulders and backs into the fight. But guys like me just count ourselves fortunate to land them without wearing out a wrist or banging a knuckle on a whirling reel handle.

A sixteen-pound, bright chum—that was my best of the week—is all the fish I need for, oh, at least fifteen minutes. When I wade back into the river after landing and releasing such a fish, I wonder, "How can I possibly top this?" As it turned out, I couldn't (not with the chums, anyway), but it was great fun to try.

There are so many salmon moving in a key July week—sometimes the kings are moving along with the chums—that you are bound to foul-hook a few. You know you have done this when a fish streaks off like an Olympic sprinter from the starting blocks, and ignores the maximum rod pressure you are able to exert. So you "just say no," point the rod at the fish, and clamp down on the line or the backing. The idea is to surrender the fly but not your line and leader.

Sometimes, though, the chum salmon fool you. Once, Hogan and I were watching Stearns wading and casting as we leaned against the beached boat and sipped cold beverages. Stearns reared back on the rod to set the hook, but it was already set, and the salmon bolted downstream, rocketing out of the water in a torpedolike broad jump that must have carried it eight feet from the eruption point to the reentry.

"Foul-hooked," Hogan called to Stearns.

Stearns grunted and shifted position as he struggled to control this runaway maniac, then called back over his shoulder, "I don't think so."

He was right. When he finally landed the fish, the fly was lodged precisely in the corner of the salmon's mouth.

"It's not often," Stearns said, panting, "that you're sort of glad a fish isn't twice its size."

The ranger who gave us our "beach speech" was a woman. She wore the plain, neat uniform of a Katmai National Park employee, and she was quite reassuring until she got to the part about her own close encounter the previous day.

"Ran into a sow and her cub on the trail," she said. "It was kind of hairy there for a minute. I just kept talking and backing away, and it turned out fine."

We had just unloaded from our float plane on the sandy beach at Brooks Camp, the fly-in outpost of cabins and other services at Brooks River, the short but world-famous flowage between two lakes in the Katmai preserve, not far from the volcanic Valley of Ten Thousand Smokes. It is a half-hour plane ride from Sarp's lodge on the Alagnak.

The ranger's job was to give us the routine drill on avoiding confrontations with the Alaska grizzly bears that gather along the Brooks to feed on spawning sockeye salmon. The description of her "hairy" meeting with two of them was less than comforting. But then, maybe it *was* comforting, after all, because she was standing there, still in possession of all her limbs and faculties.

Brooks River has been described as a zoo without bars. That's a fair-enough description, and there are two primary terrestrial specimens in this zoo: *Homo sapiens*, who come seeking fish and photographs, and *Ursus arctos*, or grizzlies, who come seeking lunch. The bigger ones can weigh upwards of 800 pounds. The idea for the human visitors is to make sure that salmon is all that's on the bears' menu.

There are some tried-and-true rules at Brooks River—codes of conduct that have been developed over decades and that prevent bloody tragedies. The rules are clearly understood by both the people and the bears (but maybe better understood by the bears). It's easy to forget that all this isn't a show put on for your benefit; these are real bears and they can kill you with one swipe of a paw. Occasionally, a fisherman becomes peeved at having to break off a salmon (the bane of the rangers are bears that get conditioned to hearing the splashes and then "steal" hooked fish) and he refuses to do so—at his peril.

One of the anglers at Katmai Lodge took the Brooks tour and came back laughing about the bear that snatched a salmon away from him. "Doggone bear had the salmon in his jaws before I could break it off," he said. "I dropped the rod and got it back later. I'm glad grizzlies don't eat graphite."

The drill at Brooks River is simple enough, although frustrating when it interferes with the fishing: Always have one person looking out for approaching bears while the rest fish. Bears always have the right-of-way. Stay at least fifty yards away from all bears, of which there may be dozens up and down the river. Some of them congregate at the famous and widely photographed Brooks Falls. Don't run from a bear—walk slowly. Don't make eye contact. Talk to the bear in normal tones and back away steadily. Talk, sing, or whistle on trails so as not to catch bears by surprise.

Though statistics would prove that you are more likely to die in a plane crash than be eaten by a bear at Brooks River (between Brooks Lake and Naknek Lake), Alaska's magnificent bears are not to be taken lightly. Upon our return to Anchorage later in the week, we read in the *Anchorage Daily News* of a six-year-old native boy killed by a grizzly farther out on the Alaska Peninsula and a woman from the lower forty-eight states being killed by a black bear in another area.

Just as awe-inspiring, in a different way, are the waves of sockeyes that find their way to the Brooks River and congregate below the falls, leaping courageously and determinedly to prolong their spawning journey. Sometimes they leap into the jaws of a bear that is perched stolidly on the lip of the lower falls as if he were a tank parked in a small creek.

Many of the anglers gather at the lower footbridge near camp headquarters, almost elbow to elbow, and occasionally a bear-spiced circus erupts. You see everything from six-weight fly rods to heavy spinning tackle and Dardevle spoons. Somebody hooks a fish, and it runs across or under adjacent lines, some of which become tangled. The more adventuresome fishermen go upstream to get away from the circus atmosphere, but they are more likely to be surprised by bears. Hovering over all of this like scoutmasters are the patrolling rangers, and while an angler respects their dedication, it is irritating at times to hear the soon-familiar words: "Bear coming! Reel in and back off." The stock joke at Brooks Camp goes like this: Two anglers are approached by a menacing looking bear, and one says to the other, "We better run." The other guy says, "You can't outrun a bear." To which the first guy replies, "No, but I can outrun *you.*"

The bears are magnificent, and the best way to approach all this is to remember that humans, anglers or otherwise, are the guests here and are not in control. Humans are interlopers in a cycle of nature that has been going on for millenniums. The sockeyes are magnificent, too, still bright from their time in the sea, and they do things on the end of a fly line that defy space, gravity, and the force of a river current. They constitute one of Alaska's greatest resources in every sense of that word—natural, commercial, and recreational.

If the bears and the salmon symbolize the wildness and power of untamed Alaska, the grayling embodies the beauty of this land. Salmon and rainbow-trout anglers, in my mind, make a mistake if they are in grayling country and do not set aside time to fish for them. There are runs and riffles where grayling are concentrated in incredible numbers, and these are the most willing of fish. We caught and released them by the dozens up in the labyrinth of winding channels known as the Alagnak Braids. Some of these side channels are so numerous and mazelike that someone who doesn't know the river could spend hours trying to find his way back to the main channel.

King, or chinook, salmon, of course, are generally considered the ultimate Alaska challenge among the salmon. They are the biggest and therefore the strongest, and the most imperial of the species. They are usually harder to find and catch, even when they are in a river in force, than the sockeyes, the chums, and the rest, but they offer the ultimate test of skill and stamina on a fly rod. There are times when they seem ridiculously easy to fool (although not necessarily to land); there are other times when they are as remote and aloof as a passing jetliner.

Once, as Stearns and I were idly waiting for our guide to cook shore lunch, I picked up a drift rod that was lying in the beached boat, walked over to the water, and made a cast with a Spin-N-Glo lure. The terminal rig had barely settled to bottom when I felt a jolt, set the hook, and was locked up with a twenty-five- to thirty-pound king salmon. I landed and released it just before the hot dogs were ready to burn.

The Alaska experience, or course, is more than the fishing itself. It is the pure thrill of blending into a vast, wild place—the remotest and most unforgiving of the still-undeveloped land that remains in the United States. The fame of rivers such as the Alagnak brings more people to their riches each year, and it is incumbent on all of us to make sure they are not degraded.

The Alaska experience is a shore lunch of just-caught salmon, charbroiled with lemon pepper and smoke-flavored with green alder leaves on the coals. (Hot dogs or hamburgers are just other options when you get tired of fish.)

The Alaska experience is passing an Indian camp and seeing the red slabs of subsistence salmon hanging on the drying poles. It is flying over the coastal mountain ranges and staring down at precipitous monoliths of ice and snow—at glaciers you know are moving but appear to be locked in time and space.

The Alaska experience is heeding the call of nature at 1 A.M., stepping outside your cabin or tent and finding that the sun is just now going down. It is seeing the fiery oranges and pastel pinks of the sunset reflected on the surface of the eternally flowing river, where the V-wakes of migrating salmon point upstream, toward their destiny and their deaths.

It is not to be missed.

CHAPTER 19

HIGH COUNTRY

JUST AS A SMALL SECTION OF POCKET WATER OR A SECONDARY-current riffle can be a microcosm of a trout stream, a small trout in a high-country creek or beaver pond can be a microcosm of what we seek when we fish. This journey with a fly rod, or whatever sporting tackle we choose, takes us to rivers, natural lakes, reservoirs, salt-water bays and flats, and sometimes even to the depths of the sea itself. But to me, the essence of the search is often found in the small waters and the small fish, which in my home state means the mountains—the high country. And often, it means brook trout, though it can also mean native cutthroat trout.

There is something about the high country and its trout that implies that the answers to meaningful mysteries are up there. One of them is the question I have been asked many times, and which I have occasionally asked of other anglers: Why do we fish? To which the reader may say to himself: Why ask why? In truth, most of us don't spend much time questioning our motives for fishing. We do it because we love it and it satisfies us, and those are reasons enough. Fishing done on any kind of ongoing basis tends to be self-revealing for anglers, and that's another reason why we do it. But from time to time, we examine the motivation a bit more deeply, if only because others who don't fish, and may even consider it cruel, are asking the question.

I once asked it (in this instance, the inquiry encompassed hunting as well as fishing) of a retired pro-football player who had accompanied me to a cornfield on the plains of eastern Colorado, where we had hunted, with some success, greater

Canada geese. On the drive home, pleasantly tired from our day, we talked of other hunts and of fishing. And I put the question to him: Why do you venture into the outdoors for these pursuits that others may say are pointless or even barbaric? And he, a big but gentle man who had grown up on a farm in South Carolina where fishing and hunting were inseparable from everyday life, paused a moment and said simply, "Because it's in me."

Of course. It may be the best answer to the why-do-you-do-it question that I ever got. Because it's in us—simple, yet profound. It is another way of saying what the great fishing writer, A. J. McClane, meant when he wrote that fishing, to a true angler, is like breathing.

But it begs a follow-up question, which is, *why* is it in us? I believe that what we seek with rod (or gun) is connection—to the wild and natural elements of life, to a time when existence was simpler, to the vibrancy of creatures that live where humans have not yet altered their world or compromised the independence of their wildness. Connection—to their beauty and honesty and tenacity and to their survival—and, thereby, a reaffirmation of the beauty of human existence and survival.

Fishing tends to level the playing field and gives us the chance to measure ourselves in a way that can't be duplicated in many of the other pursuits of our lives. We cannot compete as weekend golfers with professional golfers; we cannot match stock portfolios with Ted Turner. But a difficult fish does not come any easier to a man who has just turned a five-million-dollar profit than it does to a guy who is out of work and wondering where his next rent payment is coming from— not unless the five-million-dollar marvel happens to possess superior fishing skills. But the two men are seeking basically the same thing, I think—the satisfaction of knowing they can make the connection with this fish.

And in the high country, all these, in addition to the fish, are the things I seek. I don't go to the high country as much as I used to, for reasons that include professional practicalities (or so I tell myself) and the physical limitations brought on by advancing age. But when I return there, from time to time, I look for the small, jewellike trout in their small, jewellike waters. Somehow, the struggle of a brook trout or a cutthroat transmitted through a light fly rod at 10,000 feet or more puts me closer, in some way that is both physical and spiritual, to the essence of life. Up there, the growing season is short and the dormancy is long, and it reminds me of the relative brevity and tenuousness of my own life.

Cutthroats and brook trout are not what most people would categorize as "smart" or "selective," yet they can be moody and elusive. I have fished where the water held three-pound brook trout and found them to be among the most aloof of fish. I have seen cirque lakes at 11,000 feet, full of cutthroat trout that ignored everything offered them for hours, only to become the easiest of fish to catch when their aggressiveness was triggered by some biological or meteorological transformation that may not even be readily apparent to the angler. I have backpacked up to timberline in search of golden trout, to find that they can be impossible to catch, until finally one cast to one fish makes the connection. But I have never been disappointed in the grandeur of the high country and the fish that are able to survive there.

Along Colorado's Front Range mountains, northwest of Boulder, there is a mountain range known as the Indian Peaks, which has been designated a wilderness area. Up there, shining lakes are connected by a network of tumbling, pure brooks ("creeks" as they are called in the West). In summer, a powdery carpet of alpine snow lies upon the highest crags, where jetstream winds waft the whiteness into the thin atmosphere like wayward strands of smoke. It is high country in the fullness of its beauty. Tourists come with their backpacks and cameras to hike the trails alongside these waters, but relatively few bother to fish. It is possible to cast to rising brook trout or cutthroats and imagine that there is not another person within miles, although the camera-clutching hikers and tourists may be plodding by on a well-worn trail just out of sight and sound through the trees.

For many years, I made it a point to return at least once a summer to my favorite of these small waters, a creek that links two lakes. I always caught brook trout, occasionally a cutthroat, and it was one of the places where if I felt like it, I killed two or three fish for a meal and experienced not the least bit of conscience about it. The creek was full of brookies, and if you caught a twelve-incher, you had a fish that was a leviathan for its habitat—every bit as much a "trophy" as a six-pound brown on a brawling river.

Then the state game and fish agency decided to try an experiment in the upper lake and the connecting creek. They captured some wild reproducing rainbow trout (a rarity in the high country, which receives most of its rainbows as fingerling-size hatchery fish dumped out of airplanes) from a lake near timberline in the southwestern part of the state. They were kept alive in preparation for stocking into the lake and creek in the Indian Peaks Wilderness. Just before the biologists did that, they rotenoned the targeted section of the drainage to "get rid of" the brook trout, which would, it was felt, outcompete the rainbows.

Of course they would. They have done it time and again in countless high-elevation habitats throughout the West, sometimes to the point where all the cutthroats or other natives have disappeared and the waters are full of "stunted" brookies.

I have no quarrel with the now-successful plan in Colorado to restore native greenback cutthroat populations in key Front Range waters, even when it entailed killing existing brook-trout populations. In fact, I applauded it. The greenback, after all, is a beautiful (if somewhat fragile and vulnerably naive) fish that for many years teetered on the brink of extinction. If we lose our native trout, we have lost an aspect of our heritage.

I do have something of a quarrel, however, with the notion of some fish biologists involved in the restoration effort that the only good brookie is a dead brookie. Once, I stood flabbergasted and watched a federal biologist pitch a small brook trout caught on a fly from a greenback-restoration creek into the bushes so it wouldn't continue to "contaminate" the cutthroat project.

There are "biodiversity" freaks in this country whose idea of utopia is to set aside large blocks of land for nothing but native plant and animal species, after first running every farmer, rancher, homeowner, and nonindigenous wildlife species out of the area and letting weeds grow in the cracks in the highways. They want a grizzly behind every bush and a wolf howling on every hilltop. Everything would be in the same place it was when Eve first bit into the apple. To do anything at all inside one of these biodiversity zones, you would need a visa from God, or at least a pass from the Sierra Club.

My dictionary defines "diversity" in different terms than the rigid standards of "biodiversity." It doesn't distinguish between native and nonnative. Let's face it, folks: If we took every nonnative fish species out of every state in the country and somehow were able to put them back "where they belong," much of the sport fishing in this country would collapse. We in Colorado, for example, would be lining up for a limited number of permits to drive up to the high country and fish for native cutthroats in a limited number of places, or driving over to northwestern Colorado to fish a few rivers for whitefish. There would be no browns, rainbows, brook trout, largemouth bass, walleyes, lake trout, kokanee salmon, or a substantial list of other fish to make connections with.

So, while I understand the necessity of setting aside some waters exclusively for the restoration of native greenback trout, I cannot make the leap of faith required to endorse the eradication of one nonnative fish (the brook trout) in order to make room for another nonnative fish (the rainbow, however wild and capable of reproduction it might be). This is too much like species-supremacy tinkering to suit me.

When the brookies became absent from my favorite creek, I made myself absent from it for a number of years.

Finally, when the urge to hit the high country comes again one summer, I decide to revisit the creek. The introduced "Emerald Lake–strain" rainbows are supposed to be doing just fine, and I wanted to go up there and see how tough, or how easy, they were to catch. The word was that they were temperamental fish that didn't behave like the "dumb" rainbows you sometimes find in high-elevation waters.

I find when I get there that the beauty of my creek and its high basin, with thick forests of spruce watched over by shimmering peaks, has not changed. Some things have, though—there are even more tourists in the parking lot near the trailhead at the end of the road, and the first trout that rises to my No. 14 Adams is not a brookie, but what I have to admit, after I bring it to hand, is a handsomely colored rainbow. So are the second and the third trout, although it has taken me more than an hour of diligent stalking and casting to hook them. "Moody" is a fair description of these rainbow trout.

I move upstream to where the creek widens out over a bed of small boulders and flat rocks, bending in against an overhanging tapestry of low willow branches. It is a spot where, in bygone days, I was sure to draw rises from at least two decent-sized brook trout. They were always there, and they were usually in the nine- to twelve-inch class.

The fly line whistles back through the creek's tunnel in the spruce trees and then unfolds out in a tight loop over the upstream current, where the leader drops the Adams against the left-hand bank. The little grayish-brown dry fly bobs and drifts toward the bushy overhang, then disappears in a small splash and a flash of color. The color, however, is not the same as I had seen when the previous three fish had struck. It is darker but somehow more brilliant, and it triggers memories of a hundred strikes just like it on days that are gone but still remembered.

The fight is never in doubt, although for a minute or two the species still is. Finally, I stare down at the gleaming, spotted fish with the snail-track vermiculations on its dorsal fin and the fiery orange on its white-lined fins and decide that it is the most beautiful presence in a high-elevation world bursting with beauty.

A brook trout.

It is more than beautiful—it is a survivor. And I have made a connection with it, which by extension makes me a survivor. It had not succumbed, nor had its parentage, to the machinations of fish management and the bureaucratic decree, enforced by the technology of poison, that it was not wanted here. It did not know it was not wanted.

Ironically, it was probably here—and its brethren would continue to be here—in part because of the conservative creel limit that had been placed on the drainage to protect the introduced rainbow trout. The new regulations lowered the trout limit and imposed a size minimum, but some paper shuffler in some office somewhere must have forgotten that applying these rules to all the trout in the creek, without regard to species, would mean the conservation of not only the new rainbows, but the old brookies that had survived the rotenone and reproduced themselves.

The brookie, all nine inches of it, darts away toward the shadows of a sunken deadfall log when I release it, and I watch it go with a feeling that this fish belongs here, no matter what. If it doesn't belong here, then neither do I. And I will never entertain the thought that I don't, even when I reach those dim days at the waning of my years, when the creaking bones and the withered muscles never take me much farther than the front door.

In the meantime, I seek fish. Wherever they survive.

I seek connection.

It's in me.